Activities for the
Differentiated
Classroom

Gayle H. Gregory • Carolyn Chapman

CORWIN PRESS
Classroom

For information:

Corwin Press
A SAGE Publications Company
2455 Teller Road
Thousand Oaks, California 91320
CorwinPress.com

SAGE Publications, Ltd.
1 Oliver's Yard
55 City Road
London EC1Y 1SP
United Kingdom

SAGE Publications India Pvt. Ltd.
B 1/I 1 Mohan Cooperative
Industrial Area
Mathura Road, New Delhi
India 110 044

SAGE Publications Asia-Pacific Pvt. Ltd.
33 Pekin Street #02-01
Far East Square
Singapore 048763

Printed in the United States of America.

ISBN 978-1-4129-5344-3

This book is printed on acid-free paper.

08 09 10 11 12 10 9 8 7 6 5 4 3 2 1

Executive Editor: Kathleen Hex
Managing Developmental Editor: Christine Hood
Editorial Assistant: Anne O'Dell
Developmental Writer: Kristi Lew
Developmental Editor: Karen Hall
Proofreader: Bette Darwin
Art Director: Anthony D. Paular
Cover Designer: Monique Hahn
Interior Production Artists: Lisa Riley and Karine Hovsepian

Activities *for the* Differentiated Classroom

TABLE OF CONTENTS

Connections to Standards

This chart shows the national science standards that are covered in each chapter.

SCIENCE AS INQUIRY	Standards are covered on pages
Ability to conduct scientific inquiry.	9, 19, 58
Understand about scientific inquiry.	50, 91

PHYSICAL SCIENCE	Standards are covered on pages
Understand properties and changes of properties in matter.	32, 39
Understand motions and forces.	9, 19, 25
Understand transfer of energy.	9, 19, 25

LIFE SCIENCE	Standards are covered on pages
Understand structure and function in living systems.	76, 80
Understand reproduction and heredity.	80, 83, 86, 91
Understand populations and ecosystems.	71, 91
Understand diversity and adaptations of organisms.	71, 83, 86

EARTH AND SPACE SCIENCE	Standards are covered on pages
Understand structure of the earth system.	42, 50, 54, 58
Understand Earth's history.	45, 50
Understand Earth in the solar system.	64, 68

SCIENCE AND TECHNOLOGY	Standards are covered on pages
Identify abilities of technological design.	9, 25, 29
Understand about science and technology.	29, 91

 978-1-4129-5344-3

SCIENCE IN PERSONAL AND SOCIAL PERSPECTIVES	Standards are covered on pages
Understand the importance of personal health.	76
Understand populations, resources, and environments.	58, 71, 91
Identify natural hazards.	45, 50, 54, 58
Understand risks and benefits.	42, 50, 54, 58, 76, 91
Understand science and technology in society.	25, 29, 54, 58, 91

HISTORY AND NATURE OF SCIENCE	Standards are covered on pages
Understand science as a human endeavor.	29, 32, 64
Understand the nature of science.	29, 58, 91
Understand the history of science.	29, 50, 64

UNIFYING CONCEPTS AND PROCESSES	Standards are covered on pages
Understand systems, order, and organization.	32, 39, 45, 54, 58, 64, 68, 71, 76, 80
Understand evidence, models, and explanation.	19, 25, 32, 42, 45, 50, 54, 58, 64, 71, 80, 91
Understand change, constancy, and measurement.	19, 54
Understand evolution and equilibrium.	39, 45, 83, 86
Understand form and function.	25, 39, 54, 76

Introduction

As a teacher who has adopted the differentiated philosophy, you design instruction to embrace the diversity of the unique students in your classroom and strategically select tools to build a classroom where all students can succeed. This requires careful planning and a very large toolkit! You must make decisions about what strategies and activities best meet the needs of the students in your classroom at that time. It is not a "one size fits all" approach.

When planning for differentiated instruction, include the steps described below. Refer to the planning model in *Differentiated Instructional Strategies: One Size Doesn't Fit All, Second Edition* (Gregory & Chapman, 2007) for more detailed information.

1. Establish standards, essential questions, and expectations for the lesson or unit.

2. Identify content, including facts, vocabulary, and essential skills.

3. Activate prior knowledge. Pre-assess students' levels of readiness for the learning and collect data on students' interests and attitudes about the topic.

4. Determine what students need to learn and how they will learn it. Plan various activities that complement the learning styles and readiness levels of all students in this particular class. Locate appropriate resources or materials for all levels of readiness.

5. Apply the strategies and adjust to meet students' varied needs.

6. Decide how you will assess students' knowledge. Consider providing choices for students to demonstrate what they know.

Differentiation does not mean always tiering every lesson for three levels of complexity or challenge. It does mean finding interesting, engaging, and appropriate ways to help students learn new concepts and skills. The practical activities in this book are designed to support your differentiated lesson plans. They are not pre-packaged units, but rather activities you can incorporate into your plan for meeting the unique needs of the students in your classroom right now. Use these activities as they fit into differentiated lessons or units you are planning. They might be used for total group lessons, to reinforce learning with individuals or small groups, to focus attention, to provide additional rehearsal opportunities, or to assess knowledge. Your differentiated toolkit should be brimming with engaging learning opportunities. Take out those tools and start building success for all your students!

Put It into Practice

Differentiation is a Philosophy

For years teachers planned "the lesson" and taught it to all students, knowing that some will get it and some will not. Faced with NCLB and armed with brain research, we now know that this method of lesson planning will not reach the needs of all students. Every student learns differently. In order to leave no child behind, we must teach differently.

Differentiation is a philosophy that enables teachers to plan strategically in order to reach the needs of the diverse learners in the classroom and to help them meet the standards. Supporters of differentiation as a philosophy believe:

- All students have areas of strength.

- All students have areas that need to be strengthened.

- Each student's brain is as unique as a fingerprint.

- It is never too late to learn.

- When beginning a new topic, students bring their prior knowledge base and experience to the new learning.

- Emotions, feelings, and attitudes affect learning.

- All students can learn.

- Students learn in different ways at different times.

The Differentiated Classroom

A differentiated classroom is one in which the teacher responds to the unique needs of the students in that room, at that time. Differentiated instruction provides a variety of options to successfully reach targeted standards. It meets learners where they are and offers challenging, appropriate options for them to achieve success.

Differentiating Content By differentiating content the standards are met while the needs of the particular students being taught are considered. The teacher strategically selects the information to teach and the best resources with which to teach it using different genres, leveling materials, using a variety of instructional materials, and providing choice.

Differentiating Assessment Tools Most teachers already differentiate assessment during and after the learning. However, it is equally important to assess what knowledge or interests students bring to the learning formally or informally.

Assessing student knowledge prior to the learning experience helps the teacher find out:

- What standards, objectives, concepts, skills the students already understand

- What further instruction and opportunities for mastery are needed

- What areas of interests and feelings will influence the topic under study

- How to establish flexible groups—total, alone, partner, small group

Differentiating Performance Tasks In a differentiated classroom, the teacher provides various opportunities and choices for the students to show what they've learned. Students use their strengths to show what they know through a reflection activity, a portfolio, or an authentic task.

Differentiating Instructional Strategies When teachers vary instructional strategies and activities, more students learn content and meet standards. By targeting diverse intelligences and learning styles, teachers can develop learning activities that help students work in their areas of strength as well as areas that still need strengthening.

Some of these instructional strategies include:

- Graphic organizers

- Cubing

- Role-playing

- Centers

- Choice boards

- Adjustable assignments

- Projects

- Academic contracts

When planning, teachers in the differentiated classroom focus on the standards, but also adjust and redesign the learning activities, tailoring them to the needs of the unique learners in each classroom. Teachers also consider how the brain operates and strive to use research-based, best practices to maximize student learning. Through differentiation we give students the opportunity to learn to their full potential. A differentiated classroom engages students and facilitates learning so all learners can succeed!

CHAPTER 1

Physical Science

Energy Exchange

Standards

Science as Inquiry—Ability to conduct scientific inquiry.
Physical Science—Understand motions and forces; understand transfer of energy.
Science and Technology—Identify abilities of technological design.

Strategy
Center activity

Objectives

Students will learn about five different forms of energy: mechanical, thermal, chemical, electrical, and nuclear.
Students will discover ways to convert potential energy to kinetic energy.

Materials

My Science Portfolio reproducible
K-W-L Chart reproducible
Time Log reproducible
Resources Organizer reproducible
Star Organizer reproducible
desktop science centers (trifold foam board, construction paper pockets, task cards)
supplies for each center (as described on pages 11–12)

In this activity, students work through science centers to discover more about five different forms of energy: mechanical, thermal, chemical, electrical, and nuclear. They also apply their knowledge of potential and kinetic energy to make a domino design and a marshmallow-launching catapult.

Use the directions on pages 11–12 to set up your science centers. You may make the desktops centers by using trifold foam board and construction paper pockets, including a pocket of task cards for the directions and one or more pockets for the reproducibles. In front of each center, place a box of other supplies that students need to complete the activities.

1. Before beginning this unit, have students set up their own Science Portfolio (see page 13) using the **My Science Portfolio reproducible (page 14)**.

2. Have each student complete a **K-W-L Chart (page 15)** about energy. Prompt them to think about what they know and what they would like to know about energy and motion. Ask: *What makes things move? What forces act on things in motion?* Have students store their K-W-L Charts in their science portfolios.

3. Assign a starting point for each student to begin his or her rotation through the energy centers, or have students choose their own starting point. You may have all students complete all the center activities or assign specific activities to target readiness levels. Consider having some students work with partners or in small groups for some or all of the centers.

4. Have students complete a **Time Log (page 16)** as they work through the centers. This will help them stay on task as well as give you an ongoing assessment of what they've already done and what they still need to do.

Star Organizer Page 18

◀ 5. Have students use the **Resources Organizer (page 17)** and the **Star Organizer (page 18)** as they conduct research. Have them write the resource number (e.g., *B1, M/N1, W1*) from the Resources Organizer next to each fact recorded from that resource.

Ideas for More Differentiation

- Beginning Mastery: Have students choose a piece of playground equipment, find or draw a picture of that item, label the position of the highest potential energy, and then explain how to get the most kinetic energy.

- Approaching Mastery: Have students choose an activity that involves motion (e.g., *bicycle riding, skateboarding, surfing*) and explain how each of the following is involved in that activity: *gravity, potential energy, kinetic energy, speed, inertia, momentum.*

- High Degree of Mastery: Have students research rollercoaster design and construction and explain how each of the following is used in a rollercoaster: *gravity, potential energy, kinetic energy, speed, inertia, momentum.* Then have them draw (freehand or using computer graphics) or make a model of their own rollercoaster.

Energy Centers

Energy Center 1: Research Center

Materials: Internet access and research materials about energy (books, magazines, newspapers); Star Organizers; Resources Organizers; writing paper

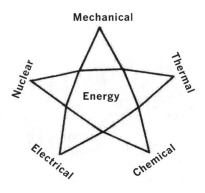

Activities:

- Define the following terms, and use a Star Organizer to record facts about them: *mechanical energy, thermal energy, chemical energy, electrical energy,* and *nuclear energy.* Write the topic *Energy* in the center of the star organizer, and write facts about each of the five forms of energy in the five points of the star. Use a Resources Organizer to keep track of the resources used.

- List the five forms of energy down the left side of a sheet of paper. As you read through newspapers and magazines articles, place a tally mark in the appropriate row every time a particular form of energy is mentioned. Make a bar graph of your results, drawing a bar for each form of energy. Summarize your bar graph.

- Find out how kinetic energy, potential energy, and gravitational potential energy are related to mechanical energy. Then write a fictional story about their relationship.

Energy Center 2: Gravitational Potential Energy

Materials: meter sticks, large and small balls, calculators

Activity:

1. Hold a meter stick vertically with one end on the ground.

2. Predict how high the larger ball will bounce when dropped from 50 cm. Then drop the ball from the 50-cm mark, and record the height of the first bounce. Repeat two more times. Find the average height of your results (average = sum/3).

3. Repeat Step 2 from the 100-cm mark. Record your results.

4. Now use the smaller ball and repeat Steps 1–3. Record your results.

5. Summarize your results. What can you conclude about gravitational potential energy and height?

Optional Challenge: Research what Sir Isaac Newton discovered about gravity. How are your results similar? How are they different?

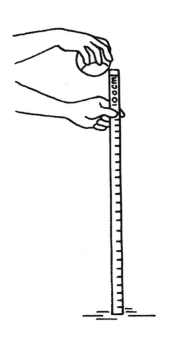

Energy Center 3: Domino Effect

Materials: several boxes of dominoes, items for building a domino obstacle course, drawing paper, pencils, stopwatch

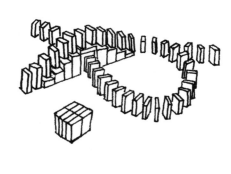

Activity:

1. Construct a domino obstacle course that can be knocked down from start to finish with a single push. Use at least 50 dominoes, and include at least one ramp and two turns in the design. You may also include other items in your obstacle course.

2. Draw a picture of your obstacle course before you test it. Below your picture, write about how you built your obstacle course, including how many dominoes you used, and explain how potential and kinetic energy will be used to knock them all down.

3. Time how long it takes for all your dominoes to fall down. You may only push the first domino in the design. If the dominoes stop falling before the end of the obstacle course, fix the problem, set up the dominoes, and start again.

Energy Center 4: Build a Catapult

Materials: Resources Organizers, references about how to build a catapult, shoe boxes, craft sticks, rubber bands, plastic spoons, marshmallows, other materials for building a catapult

Activities:

- Research and summarize how catapults are built. Use a Resources Organizer to help you keep track of your references.

- Design a catapult. Draw a picture of your catapult, indicating where it has the greatest potential energy. Then explain how that potential energy is transferred to kinetic energy.

- Use craft items to build a catapult that can propel a marshmallow. Have a catapult contest with classmates to see whose catapult works the best. After the contest, summarize your results, including the following information:

    How did you build your catapult?
    How did your catapult set the marshmallow in motion?
    Whose catapult worked the best? How do you know?
    What could you have done to make your catapult better?
    What helped your catapult work as well as it did?
    What did this activity teach you about motion and forces?

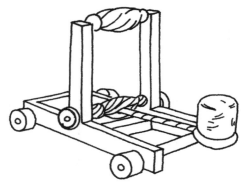

Science Portfolios

A *science portfolio* is an evolving collection of student work that supports and provides evidence of application and understanding of targeted skills and concepts throughout the year. Portfolios can help identify progress, show evidence of success, support evaluation, and demonstrate additional learning that needs to take place. They may be used to assess progress at any time to see if students are being challenged enough and show what they still need to accomplish.

The portfolios should contain evidence of growth for each science unit being taught, with samples of work being added periodically by both you and the students to show progress. Portfolios may include:

- written reports and other writing samples

- science journal or notebook

- videotapes and audiotapes of group presentations

- resource lists

- time logs

- diagrams and other graphic organizers

- illustrations and other artwork

- self-critiques and peer reviews

- teacher's notes and checklists

- selected tests, quizzes, and other pre- or post-assessments

Use the **My Science Portfolio reproducible (page 14)** to help students set up their portfolios. Portfolios may be stored in a filing cabinet or storage boxes. Each student can personalize his or her portfolio by decorating the cover.

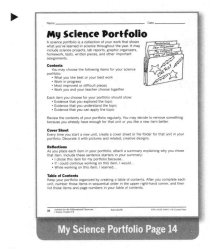

My Science Portfolio Page 14

Students should include assignments in their portfolio based on specific criteria, such as samples of their best work or favorite pieces, work that shows improvement, challenging pieces, and samples chosen by you or their peers.

An important part of the portfolio process is ongoing review, reflection, and discussion about collected work. Students should review their portfolios regularly and decide which items should remain and which should be removed. For every item students include in their portfolios, they should attach a written summary explaining why they chose that item and how it shows evidence of learning.

Allow students to share and discuss their portfolios with others. Set up individual conferences with students to help them self-critique their portfolios, evaluate progress, celebrate accomplishments, and set goals.

My Science Portfolio

A *science portfolio* is a collection of your work that shows what you've learned in science throughout the year. It may include science projects, lab reports, graphic organizers, homework, tests, written pieces, and other important assignments.

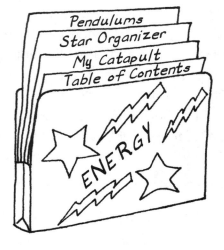

Contents

You may choose the following items for your science portfolio:
- What you like best or your best work
- Work in progress
- Most improved or difficult pieces
- Work you and your teacher choose together

Each item you choose for your portfolio should show:
- Evidence that you explored the topic
- Evidence that you understand the topic
- Evidence that you can apply the topic

Review the contents of your portfolio regularly. You may decide to remove something because you already have enough for that unit or you like a new item better.

Cover Sheet

Every time you start a new unit, create a cover sheet or file folder for that unit in your portfolio. Decorate it with pictures and related, creative designs.

Reflections

As you place each item in your portfolio, attach a summary explaining why you chose that item. Include these sentence starters in your summary:
- I chose this item for my portfolio because...
- If I could continue working on this item, I would...
- While working on this item, I learned...

Table of Contents

Keep your portfolio organized by creating a table of contents. After you complete each unit, number those items in sequential order in the upper right-hand corner, and then list those items and page numbers in your table of contents.

K-W-L Chart

Topic: _____

K What do you already **know** about this topic?	W What do you **want** to know?	L What have you **learned**? Write more facts every day to show what you've learned.

Time Log

Time Log about _____

Date	What I Worked on Today	What I Will Work on Tomorrow

Name _____ Date _____

Resources Organizer

Topic: _____

Books

Title of Book	Author	Publisher	Place of Publication	Copyright Date
1.				
2.				
3.				
4.				

Magazines/Newspapers

Title of Article	Author	Name of Periodical	Publishing Date	Article Pages
1.				
2.				
3.				
4.				

Web Sites

URL	Title	Date You Visited	Date Posted (if given)	Author (if given)
1.				
2.				
3.				
4.				

Star Organizer

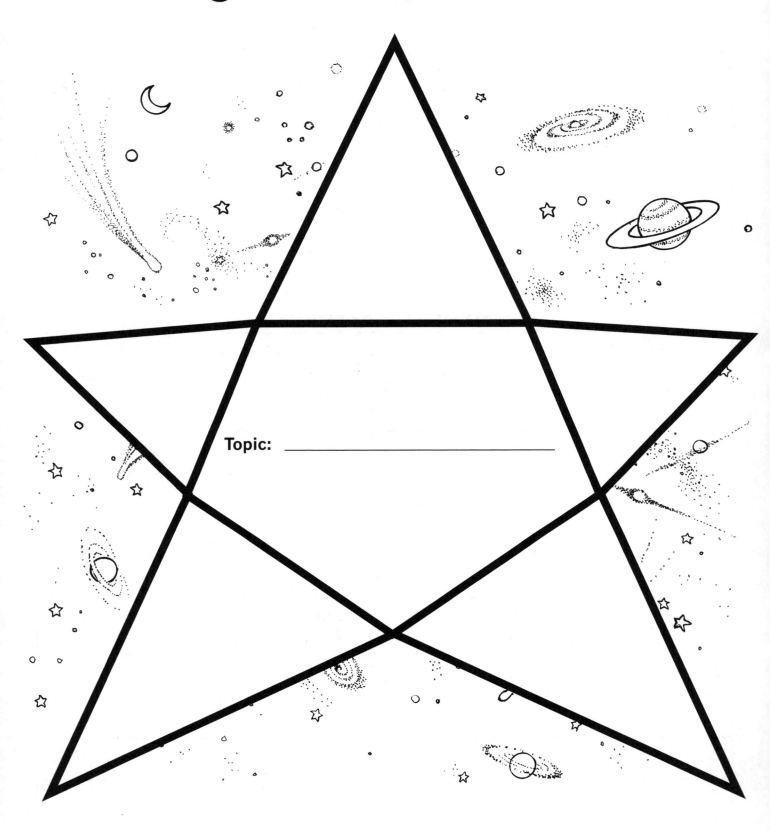

Topic: _____

Pendulums Please!

Standards
Science as Inquiry—Ability to conduct scientific inquiry.
Physical Science—Understand motions and forces; understand transfer of energy.
Unifying Concepts and Processes—Understand evidence, models, and explanation; understand change, constancy, and measurement.

Objectives
Students will identify the minimum and maximum points of potential energy and kinetic energy in a pendulum.
Students will discover that the period of a pendulum is determined by the length of the string and the force of gravity, not the weight of the bob or the starting angle.

Materials
My Science Notebook reproducibles
Pendulums Please! reproducibles
science notebooks
large washers
metric scales, meter sticks
scissors, tape
string
stopwatches or wristwatches

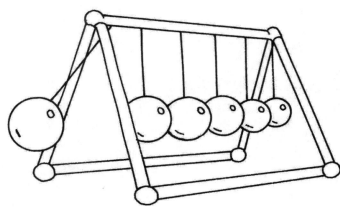

In this activity, students will design and conduct experiments to understand what determines the period (length of time for one back-and-forth swing) of a pendulum. Before they begin this activity, have students set up their science notebooks using the **My Science Notebook reproducibles (pages 21–22)**.

►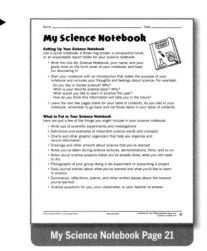

My Science Notebook Page 21

1. Activate prior knowledge by inviting students to share what they know about grandfather clocks and other machines with pendulums or swinging parts (e.g., metronomes, harmonographs, swings, cradles). Prompt students to think about the construction and movement of pendulums as well as the use of potential and kinetic energy. Create a word web on the board showing their ideas.

◄ 2. Distribute copies of the **Pendulums Please! reproducibles (pages 23–24)** to students in groups of three, and have each group conduct the pendulum experiment.

3. Monitor each group's progress as they complete the experiment. Encourage them to work cooperatively, rotating tasks, supporting each other's ideas, and checking for understanding. Remind students that they must complete their own lab write-ups but they may review their work together.

4. After students complete the experiment, invite groups to share their results. Prompt them with questions such as:

   - *What happened to the washer when you let it go?* (It swung back and forth.)
   - *What do you think gave the washer its energy?* (gravitational potential energy converting to kinetic energy)
   - *Which of these factors affects the period of the pendulum's swing: string length, starting height, or amount of weight at the bottom?* (string length)
   - *What did you notice about the starting height and the height of the initial swing?* (They were about the same.)
   - *At what two points in a pendulum's swing is potential energy the greatest?* (the highest point of the swing at each side)
   - *At what point in the swing is the energy all kinetic?* (at the bottom of the swing)
   - *What makes the pendulum swing a different number of times?* (the continuous conversion between potential gravitational energy and kinetic energy)

Ideas for More Differentiation

- Beginning Mastery: Ask students to consider what life without clocks would be like. Have them record ideas in their science notebooks.

- Approaching Mastery: Have students research and write about pendulum clocks and how to speed up a grandfather clock or about Galileo Galilei's work with pendulums.

- High Degree of Mastery: Have students research the Segway Human Transporter® to discover how the physics of the pendulum influenced its invention. Have them draw and explain a diagram to show how the Segway is an upside-down pendulum.

My Science Notebook

Setting Up Your Science Notebook

Use a spiral notebook, a three-ring binder, a composition book, or an expandable report folder for your science notebook.

- Write the title *My Science Notebook*, your name, and your grade level on the front cover of your notebook, and have fun decorating it!

- Start your notebook with an introduction that states the purpose of your notebook and includes your thoughts and feelings about science. For example:

  Do you like or dislike science? Why?
  What is your favorite science topic? Why?
  What would you like to learn in science this year?
  How do you think this information will help you in the future?

- Leave the next few pages blank for your table of contents. As you add to your notebook, remember to go back and list those items in your table of contents.

What to Put in Your Science Notebook

Here are just a few of the things you might include in your science notebook:

- Write-ups of scientific experiments and investigations
- Definitions and examples of important science words and concepts
- Charts and other graphic organizers that help you organize and record information
- Drawings and other artwork about science that you've learned
- Notes you've taken during science lectures, demonstrations, films, and so on
- Notes about science projects (what you've already done; what you still need to do)
- Photographs of your group doing a lab experiment or presenting a project
- Daily journal entries about what you've learned and what you'd like to learn in science
- Summaries, reflections, poems, and other written pieces about the science you've learned
- Science questions for you, your classmates, or your teacher to answer

My Science Notebook (cont.)

Recording Scientific Experiments and Investigations

When conducting an experiment or investigation, record the following information:

- **Title of the Experiment**—Written at the top of your notebook paper or record sheet

- **Purpose**—Written in the form of a scientific question that you want to investigate (Example: *What can affect the speed and momentum of a pendulum?*)

- **Hypothesis**—Your prediction of the outcome of the experiment; something that can be tested (Example: *If I use a longer string, the pendulum will swing slower.*)

- **Materials**—Listed in the order of use

- **Procedure**—Step-by-step directions about how to do the experiment; it may also include a picture or diagram of the setup

- **Results**—Data and observations (charts, graphs, pictures, and so on)

- **Analysis of Results**—Looking at patterns and trends in your data; seeing if your results support your hypothesis

- **Conclusion**—A statement about what you have learned from the experiment, which may also lead to new questions and follow-up investigations

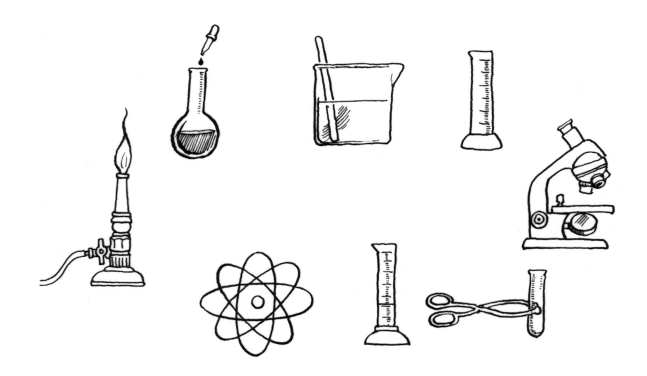

Pendulums Please!

Directions: Work with two other students to complete this activity. Record the information in your science notebook.

Materials

metric scale	meter stick
washers	desk or table
string	tape
scissors	stopwatch or wristwatch
tape	

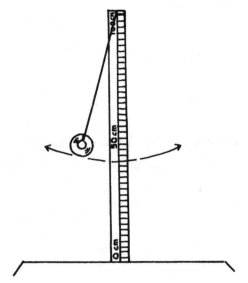

Procedure

1. Use a metric scale to measure the mass of one washer. Record that mass in your notebook.

2. Tie the washer to the end of a string.

3. Cut the string to a length of 63 cm.

4. Tape a meterstick vertically against the side of a desk or table. Then tape the string to the top of the meter stick, leaving 60 cm of the string and the washer hanging down to create a pendulum.

5. Hold the pendulum off to one side at about a 45-degree angle, and measure the height of that starting position.

6. Assign the following roles to your group: Measurer, Counter, Timer. When you let go of the pendulum,
   - The Measurer reads the height of the initial swing.
   - The Counter counts the number of swings back and forth.
   - The Timer announces when 15 seconds have passed.

   Record your results in your notebooks.

7. Reduce the length of the string by half, and repeat the experiment. First predict what will happen. Then switch roles, and test to see if you are correct. Record your results.

8. Complete one or more of the following extension activities. Change only one variable of the experiment at a time. Predict (hypothesize) what will happen to the swinging motion (height and number of strings). Then test and check. Record your observations and results.

Pendulums Please! (cont.)

More to Explore

What if you:

- Use a longer string? a shorter string?
- Use more than one washer?
- Start the pendulum from a higher position? a lower position?
- Want the pendulum to swing back and forth one time in exactly five seconds? How would you do it? Plan, test, and check.

Analysis and Conclusion

1. What happened to the washer when you let it go?

_____

_____

2. What do you think gave the washer its energy?

_____

3. Which of these three factors affects the period of the pendulum's swing: the length of the string, the starting height, the amount of weight at the bottom?

_____

4. What did you notice about the starting height and the height of the initial swing?

_____

5. At what two points in a pendulum's swing is the potential energy the greatest?

_____

6. At what point in the swing is the energy all kinetic energy?

_____

7. What makes the pendulum swing a different number of times?

_____

8. Summarize your results in your science notebook, and write a conclusion. Compare your results and conclusion with those from three other groups. How are your results and conclusion alike? How are they different? Why do you think so?

KISS: Keep It Simple, Silly!

Standards

Physical Science—Understand motions and forces; understand transfer of energy.

Science and Technology—Identify abilities of technological design.

Science in Personal and Social Perspectives—Understand science and technology in society.

Unifying Concepts and Processes—Understand evidence, models, and explanation; understand form and function.

Objective

Students will design and build a creative machine that consists of two or more simple machines.

Materials

K-W-L Chart reproducible
KISS Expert Investigation reproducible
Resources Organizer reproducible
KISS Construction Guide reproducible
Time Log reproducible
picture of a simple machine
video recorder (optional)
science notebooks

Strategies

Jigsaw

Open-ended project

All mechanical devices are comprised of one or more simple machines: inclined plane, lever and fulcrum, wedge, wheel and axle, screw, or pulley. In this activity, students design and construct a Rube Goldberg-type device using as many simple machines as they can.

A Rube Goldberg machine, named after cartoonist Reuben Goldberg, is any exceedingly complex apparatus or device that performs simple tasks in an indirect, convoluted way. The device typically has a least ten steps and includes an unexpected aspect, such as the comical devices used in the *Home Alone* movies. The Hasbro game *Mousetrap* also features these gadgets.

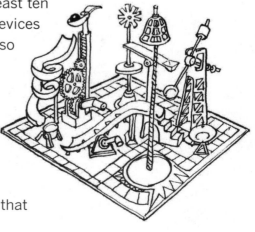

1. Show a picture of a simple machine, and have students explain the machine's use in their lives. Then ask them to identify the difference between a simple machine and a complex machine. List examples of complex machines used at home.

2. Discuss Rube Goldberg machines, and explain to students that they will work in groups to create their own machine.

Kiss Expert Investigation Page 27

Kiss Construction Guide Page 28

3. "Jigsaw" students to learn more about each simple machine:

   a. Place students in base groups of six, and assign each student a simple machine.

   b. Have students fill out a **K-W-L Chart (page 15)** about what they know and would like to know about their machine.

   c. Then have students form expert groups (groups of students with the same assignment) and complete the **KISS Expert Investigation reproducible (page 27)** using research materials to learn more about their simple machine. Have them use a **Resources Organizer (page 17)** to keep track of their resources.

   d. When students have completed the KISS Expert worksheet, have them return to their base group to teach other members what they learned about their simple machine.

4. Now have student teams design and create their own Rube Goldberg machine using the **KISS Construction Guide (page 28)**. Circle one of the tasks, and have all students build a machine that does the same thing. Or, let individual teams decide which tasks they will do.

5. Students will need a least one week to complete this project. Have students use a **Time Log (page 16)** to keep them on task and provide you with an ongoing assessment of their progress.

6. Have teams participate in a Contraption Contest to show how their finished machines work. A few days before the contest, ask teams to turn in a written description and a sketch of their machine to make sure all rules were followed. If possible, videotape the contest, and award certificates to all participants.

Ideas for More Differentiation

- Beginning Mastery: Have students list the six simple machines, look for examples of each simple machine, and write down an example of each one. Then have them explain how each simple machine is used in daily life.

- Approaching Mastery: Have students explain how simple machines help do work. Have them include the following terms: *friction, load, force, surface area, distance*.

- High Degree of Mastery: Have students research the life and inventions of Leonardo da Vinci. Ask them to find a photograph or diagram of one of his inventions and explain how each machine is used.

KISS Expert Investigation

Type of Simple Machine: _____

Part 1
Explain what your simple machine does and how it works. Use at least two different resources to help you define and explain your machine. Include at least one picture.

Build a model of your simple machine or find an example to show your teammates.

Part 2
Find a larger, more complex machine that includes your simple machine. Explain how the complex machine works, and include a labeled diagram of it. Bring the machine to class if possible, take a photograph of it, or build a model to show your teammates.

Resources: _____

_____

KISS Construction Guide

Step 1: Learn more about Rube Goldberg machines. Then brainstorm ideas for your own creative contraption that includes as many simple machines as possible.

inclined plane

lever

wedge

screw

pulley

wheel and axle

- Your machine must perform at least one of the following tasks:
  Move an empty can at least 0.5 m
  Turn on a power switch
  Strum a guitar
  Keep someone awake in class
  Put blush on a doll's cheeks
  Shut off an alarm clock
  Sharpen a pencil
  Put a stamp on a letter
  Crack an egg into a frying pan
  Task of your choice (with teacher's approval):

  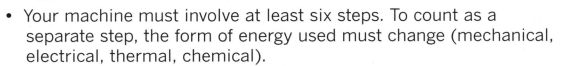

- Your machine must involve at least six steps. To count as a separate step, the form of energy used must change (mechanical, electrical, thermal, chemical).

- It must include at least three different types of simple machines, but you can use them as many times as needed.

- It can start in any way, but you should not have to use excessive force to start it. After your machine starts, you shouldn't have to touch it again.

- You cannot include anything that is dangerous or harmful. You cannot use any flame larger than a candle flame or any electricity that is not supplied by a battery.

Step 2: Sketch a picture and write a description of your machine before you begin construction. Identify all energy conversions. Brainstorm possible materials you can use, and decide who on your team will provide those materials.

Step 3: Get your teacher's approval, and gather all of your supplies before you begin construction. Write step-by-step directions on how to build your machine. Decide together who will be responsible for each part of the machine.

Step 4: Work together to build your machine. Draw pictures or take photographs of your machine as you build it and after you complete it.

Step 5: Test your machine to make sure it works consistently. Then get ready to compete in a Contraption Contest. The winning contraption will have the most simple machines and the most steps that successfully completes the task.

Invention Extension

Standards
Science and Technology—Identify abilities of technological design; understand about science and technology.
Science in Personal and Social Perspectives—Understand science and technology in society.
History and Nature of Science—Understand science as a human endeavor; understand the nature of science; understand the history of science.

Objective
Students will develop and create their own invention to solve a modern-day problem.

Materials
Invention Extension reproducible
index cards
poster board, markers, and other supplies for creating a poster
video recorder (optional)

Throughout history, many innovative people have created ways to make our lives easier. These individuals had vision, determination, deductive reasoning, creativity, and persistence. In this activity, students will research some of these amazing inventors and devise their own invention to solve a current problem.

1. Help students focus for the activity. Ask: *What do you think cave people were thinking when they invented the wheel? What purpose did it serve?* Then pair up students into "energizing partners" to brainstorm a list of useful inventions and their inventors. Have partners share their ideas and point out any similarities and differences.

2. Write the names of inventors (see page 30 for suggestions) on index cards, and have each student pair randomly select a card. Or, have students choose their own inventor from a list on the board. Then have partners research the inventor and create a poster about him or her. The posters should answer the five Ws (*who, when, where, what, why*) and include at least one picture of the inventor and the invention.

- Virgie Ammons
- Alexander Graham Bell
- Tim Berners-Lee
- Josephine Cochran
- Michael Faraday
- Lillian Moller Gilbreth
- Beulah Henry
- Eli Whitney

- Mary Anderson
- Bessie Blount
- Thomas Edison
- Benjamin Franklin
- Sarah Goode
- Guglielmo Marconi
- The Wright brothers
- James Watt

3. Have partners present their poster to the class, describing and explaining each part of the poster. Encourage classmates to ask questions and assess each presentation.

Invention Extension Page 31

4. Distribute copies of the **Invention Extension reproducible (page 31)**, and tell students they will create another presentation, this time about themselves as inventors. Students may work by themselves, with a partner, or in small groups to create an invention that solves a current problem. They may choose any kind of presentation, such as multimedia, drama, animation, puppetry, diorama, or mural. As they brainstorm ideas for their inventions, encourage them to think about what they've learned from the poster presentations and what kinds of things they use every day.

5. Videotape students' presentations and/or invite parents to be part of the audience.

Ideas for More Differentiation

- Beginning Mastery: Ask students to make a list of five inventions they use every day and find out when they were invented and who invented them.

- Approaching Mastery: Have students research the history of computers and use a graphic organizer to compare and contrast early computers to those we use today.

- High Degree of Mastery: Ask students to imagine what American culture will be like 50 years from now and predict what new inventions might appear. Have them write a short story or draw a cartoon showing a futuristic city and pointing out all the new inventions.

Invention Extension

Directions: Create an invention that will solve a problem in our society. You may work independently, with a partner, or in a small group to complete this assignment.

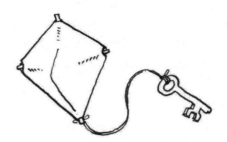

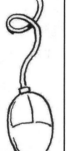

1. Generate a list of inventions that could resolve one or more of the following problems. Use your imagination. Discuss your ideas.
   - pollution
   - aging
   - health
   - recreation
   - traffic
   - literacy
   - clean energy source
   - weather protection
   - food shortage
   - any other topic of public interest

2. Choose one of your ideas, and sketch your invention. Summarize how it works and whom it will benefit. Get your teacher's approval before continuing on to the next step.

3. Plan a presentation that is at least five minutes long. Describe your invention, how it works, and how it will be used. You may choose any kind of presentation (with teacher approval)—multimedia, drama, animation, puppetry, diorama, model.

4. Present your invention to the class. Remember to speak slowly and clearly. Leave time for your audience to ask questions.

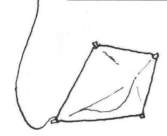

It's Periodic

Strategy
Game

Standards

Physical Science—Understand properties and changes of properties in matter.

History and Nature of Science—Understand science as a human endeavor.

Unifying Concepts and Processes—Understand systems, order, and organization; understand evidence, models, and explanation.

Objective

Students will create a game about the periodic table.

Materials

Periodic Table Organizer reproducibles
Periodic Table Game reproducible
Periodic Table reproducibles
Project Review reproducible
colored pencils or highlighters
scissors
resealable plastic bags

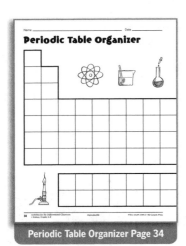

Periodic Table Organizer Page 34

1. Distribute copies of the **Periodic Table Organizer (pages 34–35)**. Ask students: *What does this organizer show?* (an incomplete periodic table) *What belongs in each box?* (symbol of the element, name of the element, atomic number, atomic mass)

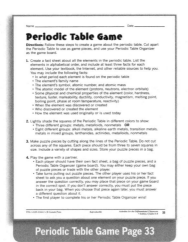

Periodic Table Game Page 33

2. Then distribute copies of the **Periodic Table Game reproducible (page 33)**, the **Periodic Table reproducibles (page 36–37)**, and other supplies for the game. Read the directions with students, and encourage more advanced learners to create their own modified version of the game.

3. Provide time for students to play their game. Invite groups to rotate to play different versions of the game. After each rotation, have them complete a **Project Review reproducible (page 38)**.

Ideas for More Differentiation

Have pairs of students work together to create only one set of puzzle pieces for the Periodic Table Game, with each player gathering facts for only one half of the elements and building only the right or left half of the table.

Periodic Table Game

Directions: Follow these steps to create a game about the periodic table. Cut apart the Periodic Table to use as game pieces, and use your Periodic Table Organizer as the game board.

1. Create a fact sheet about all the elements in the periodic table. List the elements in alphabetical order, and include at least three facts for each element. Use your textbook, the Internet, and other reliable sources to help you. You may include the following facts:
   • In what period each element is found on the periodic table
   • The element's family name
   • The element's symbol, atomic number, and atomic mass
   • The atomic model of the element (protons, neutrons, electron orbitals)
   • Some physical and chemical properties of the element (color, hardness, texture, luster, malleability, ductility, conductivity, magnetism, melting point, boiling point, phase at room temperature, reactivity)
   • When the element was discovered or created
   • Who discovered or created the element
   • How the element was used originally or is used today

2. Lightly shade the squares of the Periodic Table in different colors to show:
   • Three different groups: metals, metalloids, nonmetals **OR**
   • Eight different groups: alkali metals, alkaline earth metals, transition metals, metals in mixed groups, lanthanides, actinides, metalloids, nonmetals

3. Make puzzle pieces by cutting along the lines of the Periodic Table. Do not cut across any of the squares. Each piece should be from three to seven squares in size. Include a variety of shapes and sizes. Store your puzzle pieces in a bag.

4. Play the game with a partner.
   • Each player should have their own fact sheet, a bag of puzzle pieces, and a Periodic Table Organizer (game board). You may either keep your own bag of puzzle pieces or trade with the other player.
   • Take turns pulling out puzzle pieces. The other player uses his or her fact sheet to ask you a question about one element on your puzzle piece. If you answer the question correctly, you may place that piece on your game board in the correct spot. If you don't answer correctly, you must put the piece back in your bag. When you choose that piece again later, you must answer a different question about it.
   • The first player to complete his or her Periodic Table Organizer wins!

Periodic Table Organizer

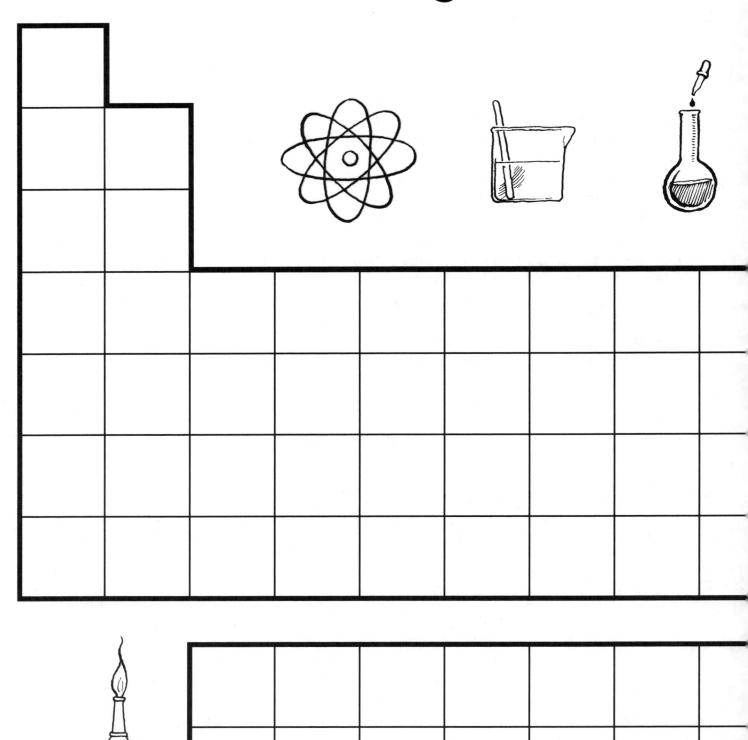

 Activities for the Differentiated Classroom
• *Science, Grades 6–8*   Reproducible   978-1-4129-5344-3 • © Corwin Press

Periodic Table Organizer

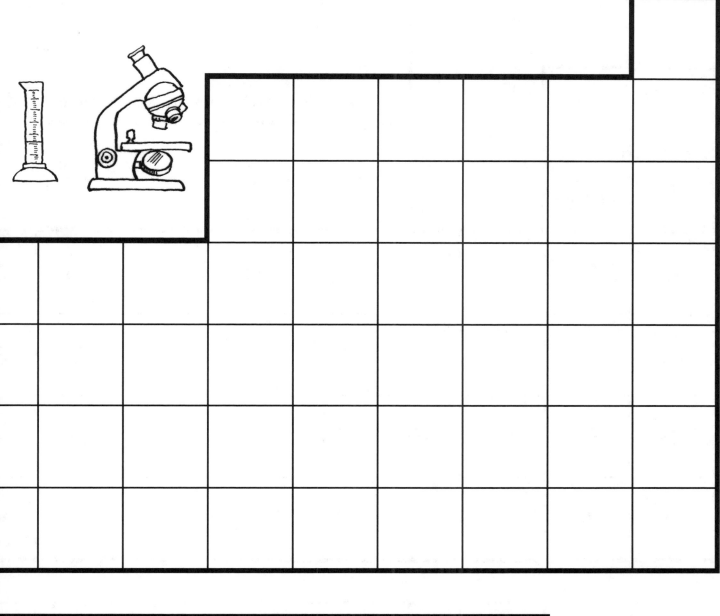

Periodic Table

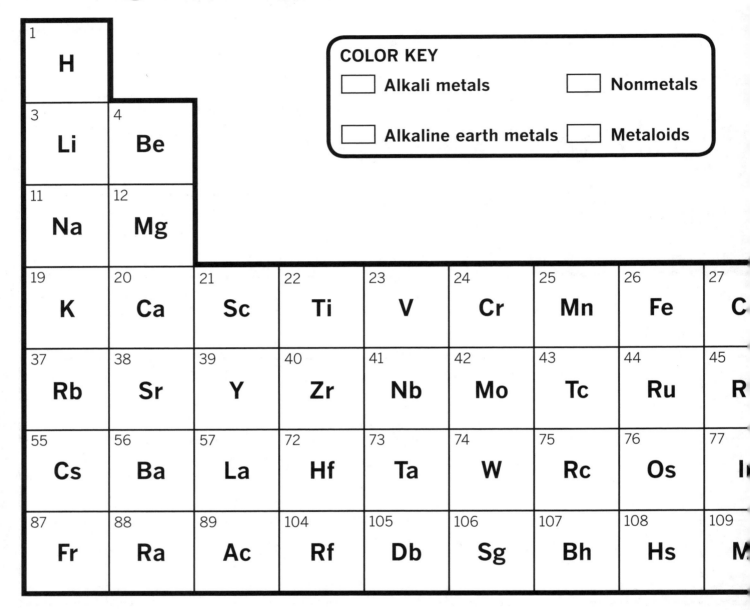

COLOR KEY

☐ Alkali metals   ☐ Nonmetals

☐ Alkaline earth metals   ☐ Metaloids

1 H								
3 Li	4 Be							
11 Na	12 Mg							
19 K	20 Ca	21 Sc	22 Ti	23 V	24 Cr	25 Mn	26 Fe	27 C
37 Rb	38 Sr	39 Y	40 Zr	41 Nb	42 Mo	43 Tc	44 Ru	45 R
55 Cs	56 Ba	57 La	72 Hf	73 Ta	74 W	75 Rc	76 Os	77 I
87 Fr	88 Ra	89 Ac	104 Rf	105 Db	106 Sg	107 Bh	108 Hs	109 M

58 Ce	59 Pr	60 Nd	61 Pm	62 Sm	63 Eu	64 G
90 Th	91 Pa	92 U	93 Np	94 Pu	95 Am	96 C

Periodic Table

					2 He
5 B	6 C	7 N	8 O	9 F	10 Ne
13 Al	14 Si	15 P	16 S	17 Cl	18 Ar

Ni	29 Cu	30 Zn	31 Ga	32 Ge	33 As	34 Se	35 Br	36 Kr
Pd	47 Ag	48 Cd	49 In	50 Sn	51 Sb	52 Te	53 I	54 Xe
Pt	79 Au	80 Hg	81 Tl	82 Pb	83 Bi	84 Po	85 At	86 Rn
Ds	111 Rg	112 Uub	113 Uut	114 Uup	115 Uuq	116 Uuh	117 Uus	118 Uuo

b	66 Dy	67 Ho	68 Er	69 Tm	70 Yb	71 Lu
Bk	98 Cf	99 Es	100 Fm	101 Md	102 No	103 Lr

Name ______________________________ Date ______________

Project Review

Name of project: ______________________________

Completed by: ______________________________

Name of reviewer (your name): ______________________________

Directions: Evaluate the project. Circle a score for each category.

Use of information	1	2	3	4	5
Accuracy of information	1	2	3	4	5
Visual appeal	1	2	3	4	5
Overall presentation	1	2	3	4	5

What did you like best about this project?

____

____

What did you like the least?

____

____

How would you improve the project?

____

____

Other comments or questions:

____

____

____

____

978-1-4129-5344-3 • © Corwin Press

Bonding Buddies

Standards
Physical Science—Understand properties and changes of properties in matter.
Unifying Concepts and Processes—Understand systems, order, and organization; understand evolution and equilibrium; understand form and function.

Objective
Students will learn how atoms bond to form chemical compounds.

Materials
Bonding Buddies reproducible
Periodic Table of the Elements
index cards or squares of construction paper
colored pencils or thin markers
paper clips

The smallest particle of any element is called an *atom*, a positively charged nucleus of *protons* surrounded by negatively charged *electrons* orbiting in concentric spherical shells (according to the Bohr model). In a neutral atom, the number of electrons and protons is the same (as indicated by its *atomic number*). But when combining with other atoms to form a *molecule*, an atom will gain or lose electrons in order to attain a stable configuration and fill its outermost shell of electrons (*valence shell*). When this happens, the atom is a charged *ion*.

Atoms of nonmetals, such as chlorine, gain electrons to complete their valence shell, giving them a negative charge (*anions*). Atoms of metals, such as potassium, lose electrons. The shell below the valence shell becomes part of the completed outermost shell, resulting in atoms with positive charge (*cations*).

The rows of a Periodic Table of the Elements indicate which valence shell is being filled (each row begins a new valence shell of electrons), whereas the columns of a periodic table indicate how many electrons are in that outermost shell. Metallic ions from Column 1 of the periodic table tend to lose one electron for stability, giving them a net +1 charge. Ions from Column 2 tend to lose two electrons, resulting in a net +2 charge. Nonmetallic ions from Column 16 tend to gain two electrons to fill their valence shell, resulting in a net −2 charge, whereas those from Column 17 tend to gain one electron, resulting in a −1 charge.

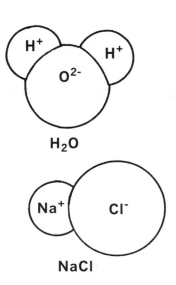

H_2O

NaCl

1. Post a Periodic Table of the Elements where students can see it. Write ionic charges *1+, 2+, 3+, 3–, 2–, 1–* in a row on the board, and work with students to generate a list of elements under each one. For example: *(1+) Hydrogen H+, Lithium Li+, Sodium Na+, Potassium K+; (2+) Beryllium Be^{2+}, Magnesium Mg^{2+}, Calcium Ca^{2+}; (3+) Boron B^{3+}, Aluminum Al^{3+}; (3–) Nitride N^{3-}, Phosphide P^{3-}; (2–) Oxygen O^{2-}, Sulfide S^{2-}; (1–) Fluoride F$^-$, Chloride Cl$^-$, Bromide B$^-$, Iodide I$^-$*. Point out that the names of anions usually end with *–ide*.

2. Give each student ten index cards (or paper squares). Have students write the symbol and name of an ion on each card to make ionic-charge cards. They may choose any ion (cation or anion) and use the same ion more than once. Students will "bond" their ions with their classmates' to form neutral compounds. For example, an oxygen ion *O^{2-}* can bond with a cation with a 2+ charge, such as *Mg^{2+}* to form *MgO*. Or, it can bond with two 1+ cations, such as two *H+* to form *H$_2$O*. Students may only form compounds with one kind of cation and one kind of anion.

3. Have students write their name on the back of each card and paperclip the cards together to form compounds. They may use their cards for either the cation or the anion, not both.

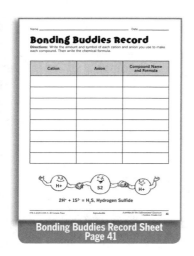

Bonding Buddies Record Sheet
Page 41

4. Distribute copies of the **Bonding Buddies Record Sheet (page 41)**, and review how to complete the chart (*2 H+ + 1 S^{2-} = H$_2$S, hydrogen sulfide*). Give students 15 minutes to find bonding buddies and make as many compounds as they can. Have them record each compound and give you the cards. Remind them that the positive ion is written first.

5. Discuss the results with students. Check each set of cards to see if students successfully formed neutral compounds.

Ideas for More Differentiation

• Have students use magnetic letters/numbers to practice writing chemical formulas, such as *NaCl, KCl, HCl*, and *CaCl$_2$*.

• Have students go online to see if their compounds truly exist. Have them write how the compounds are used in real life.

• Have students draw a picture of each ion (an electron configuration) on the back of their ionic-charge cards, and then draw pictures on the back of their record sheet to show how ionic bonding occurs to form each compound.

Bonding Buddies Record

Directions: Write the amount and symbol of each cation and anion you use to make each compound. Then write the chemical formula.

Cation	Anion	Compound Name and Formula

$2H^+ + 1S^{2-} = H_2S$, **Hydrogen Sulfide**

CHAPTER 2

Earth Science

My Trip as a Drip

Strategy
Choice board

Standards

Earth and Space Science—Understand structure of the earth system.
Science in Personal and Social Perspectives—Understand risks
and benefits.
Unifying Concepts and Processes—Understand evidence, models,
and explanation.

Objectives

Students will identify and describe parts of the water cycle, including
alternative pathways.
Students will apply knowledge of the water cycle by writing a creative
story about a water droplet.

Materials

My Trip as a Drip reproducible
science notebooks
dice

Our hydrosphere consists of all water found on, under, and over the
surface of Earth. The movement of water in the hydrosphere is called the
water cycle. The water cycle is often depicted as a circular pathway—
water evaporating from the ocean, condensing into clouds, precipitating
onto land, and then flowing back into the ocean to repeat the process
again. While this is one path that a water droplet may take, it is not
the only way water gets from one location to another. In this activity,
students learn that there are a number of alternative routes water can
take as it travels through the water cycle.

1. Have students answer the following questions in their science
   notebooks: *Where is water found on Earth? Where does water come
   from? How does water get from one place to another on Earth?*
   Have students discuss their answers with a partner before sharing
   their answers aloud. Prompt students to identify parts of the water
   cycle and name different places where water is found (*glaciers,
   oceans, river, lakes, clouds, soil, plants, animals, and groundwater*).
   Help them understand that the water we drink has to come from

somewhere else. When our bodies are finished using the water, it will be used another way in the water cycle. This is also a good opportunity to discuss how water pollution can affect the water cycle and the planet as a whole.

2. Distribute copies of **My Trip as a Drip reproducible (page 44)**, and explain to students that they will be describing a water droplet traveling though the water cycle. Show students how to choose one task from this choice board to complete. Allow adequate time for students to complete the project.

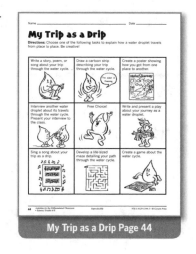

My Trip as a Drip Page 44

3. Invite students to share their finished products with the class. Encourage peers to ask questions and provide feedback about each presentation.

Ideas for More Differentiation

- Beginning Mastery: Have students list and compare the different ways living things (plants, animals, humans) depend on water every day.

- Approaching Mastery: Have students discuss what would happen to a community if its water supply became contaminated. Have them research a source of water pollution in their community and propose a way to eliminate that source of pollution.

- High Degree of Mastery: Have students research the instruments used to measure rainfall and how scientists use cloud seeding to produce rain during droughts. Have them write a report about their findings and/or present a demonstration of these methods.

My Trip as a Drip

Directions: Choose one of the following tasks to explain how a water droplet travels from place to place. Be creative!

Write a story, poem, or song about your trip through the water cycle. 	Draw a cartoon strip describing your trip through the water cycle. 	Create a poster showing how you got from one place to another. 
Interview another water droplet about its travels through the water cycle. Present your interview to the class. 	Free Choice! 	Write and present a play about your journey as a water droplet. 
Sing a song about your trip as a drip. 	Develop a life-sized maze detailing your path through the water cycle. 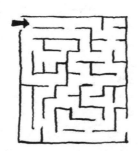	Create a game about the water cycle. 

Ancient History

Standards
Earth and Space Science—Understand Earth's history.
Science in Personal and Social Perspectives—Identify natural hazards.
Unifying Concepts and Processes—Understand systems, order, and organization; understand evidence, models, and explanation; understand evolution and equilibrium.

Strategies
Cooperative group learning

Project

Objective
Students will explore Earth's geological timeline using models.

Materials
Time Log reproducible
Resources Organizer reproducible
Origins of Life reproducible
Mass Reduction or Extinction reproducible
The Changing Planet reproducible
chart paper
science notebooks
large self-stick notes, tape
supplies for team projects (See Phase 4, page 46)

The geologic time scale is a system that divides Earth's 4.6 billion years of geological history into four eras: Precambrian, Paleozoic, Mesozoic, and Cenozoic. In order to understand fossil evidence for evolution, students must grasp the immensity of the geologic time scale. In this activity, students complete a multitask project about Earth's history.

1. Write the following 15 time periods at the top of separate sheets of chart paper. Post them in sequence around the classroom.

   Precambrian Era

Paleozoic Era	Mesozoic Era	Cenozoic Era
a. Cambrian period	a. Triassic period	a. Tertiary period
b. Ordovician period	b. Jurassic period	b. Quaternary period
c. Silurian period	c. Cretaceous period	(present time)
d. Devonian period		
e. Carboniferous period		
f. Permian period		

2. Have students record in their notebooks what they already know and want to know about each period. Ask them to share their ideas.

3. Have students work in groups to complete a long-term project about Earth's geological history. Remind them to share the responsibilities equally when assigning parts. Have students use a **Time Log (page 16)**, a **Resources Organizer (page 17)**, and their science notebooks to track their progress.

Phase 1

Assign two or three students to each chart. Have teams use at least three resources to determine the time span for their geological period and write a one-paragraph summary about its most notable events. Check students' work before they complete the top half of the chart.

Phase 2

◄ Divide the class into three groups. Give one group copies of the **Origins of Life reproducible (page 47)**; the second group, the **Mass Reduction or Extinction**
◄ **reproducible (page 48)**; and the third group, **The Changing Planet reproducible (page 49)**. Have groups cut apart the cards, conduct research to complete the cards, tape the cards to large self-stick notes, and stick them to the correct charts below the summaries. Check students' work for accuracy. (See Answer Key on page 95.)

Phase 3

Assign new partners to each chart, and have them put the self-stick notes in chronological order. Have them draw or find pictures to go with the notes to create a mini-timeline.

Phase 4

Have students sign up for one of the following projects and work together to complete the assignment. Ask them to refer to the information on the charts.

- Create a four-tiered board game including all four geological eras.
- Create a video about a time traveler in a time machine. Include all four eras.
- Create a diorama timeline with each diorama representing a different geological period.
- Create a giant pop-up book about Earth's geological history.
- Create a PowerPoint® presentation about major geological events that shaped Earth, such as the ice ages, volcanic and tectonic activity, comets, meteorites, and asteroids.

Origins of Life Page 47

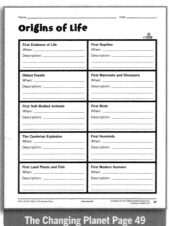

The Changing Planet Page 49

Name _____ Date _____

Origins of Life

First Evidence of Life

When: _____

Description: _____

_____

_____

Oldest Fossils

When: _____

Description: _____

_____

_____

First Soft-Bodied Animals

When: _____

Description: _____

_____

_____

The Cambrian Explosion

When: _____

Description: _____

_____

_____

First Land Plants and Fish

When: _____

Description: _____

_____

_____

First Reptiles

When: _____

Description: _____

_____

_____

First Mammals and Dinosaurs

When: _____

Description: _____

_____

_____

First Birds

When: _____

Description: _____

_____

_____

First Hominids

When: _____

Description: _____

_____

_____

First Modern Humans

When: _____

Description: _____

_____

_____

Mass Reduction or Extinction

Single-Celled, Soft-Bodied Animals

When they declined: _____

Description: _____

_____

_____

˜50% of Marine Invertebrates

When they declined: _____

Description: _____

_____

_____

Reef-Builders, Shallow-Water Organisms

When they declined: _____

Description: _____

_____

_____

Dinosaurs, 60–80% of All Species

When they declined: _____

Description: _____

_____

_____

˜25% of Marine Invertebrate Families

When they declined: _____

Description: _____

_____

_____

Foraminifera, Gastropods, Sea Urchins

When they declined: _____

Description: _____

_____

_____

˜50% of Marine Invertebrate Genera

When they declined: _____

Description: _____

_____

_____

Plant-Eating Woodland Herbivores

When they declined: _____

Description: _____

_____

_____

˜90% of All Species

When they declined: _____

Description: _____

_____

_____

Mammals and Birds Over 45 lbs.

When they declined: _____

Description: _____

_____

_____

The Changing Planet

The Great Oceans Form

When: _____

Description: _____

_____

_____

Great Mountain Ranges Form

When: _____

Description: _____

_____

_____

Continents Begin Shifting

When: _____

Description: _____

_____

_____

Pangaea Supercontinent Forms

When: _____

Description: _____

_____

_____

Rodinia Supercontinent Forms

When: _____

Description: _____

_____

_____

Pangaea Supercontinent Breaks Up

When: _____

Description: _____

_____

_____

Rodinia Supercontinent Breaks Up

When: _____

Description: _____

_____

_____

Inland Seas Dry Up

When: _____

Description: _____

_____

_____

Gondwana Forms

When: _____

Description: _____

_____

_____

Global Ice Ages Begin

When: _____

Description: _____

_____

_____

Shifting Plates

Strategies

Choice board

Open-ended project

Standards

Science as Inquiry—Understand about scientific inquiry.
Earth and Space Science—Understand structure of the earth system; understand Earth's history.
Science in Personal and Social Perspectives—Identify natural hazards; understand risks and benefits.
History and Nature of Science—Understand the history of science.
Unifying Concepts and Processes—Understand evidence, models, and explanation.

Objective

Students will create projects that show their understanding of plate tectonics and the formation of Earth's land features.

Materials

K-W-L Chart reproducible
Shifting Plates: World Map reproducible
Shifting Plates: Choice Boards reproducible
Time Log reproducible
Resources Organizer reproducible
Project Review reproducible
scissors, glue
science notebooks
markers and colored pencils
Internet access and other resources about plate tectonics, earthquakes, and volcanoes

Earth's outer shell, or *lithosphere*, is not one solid piece. It's broken up like a cracked eggshell into huge pieces (our continents) and many smaller pieces called *tectonic plates*. The continual movement of these plates causes two types of disturbances—earthquakes and volcanoes. In this activity, students explore what the interior of Earth looks like, the theory of plate tectonics, and how these plates cause earthquakes and volcanoes.

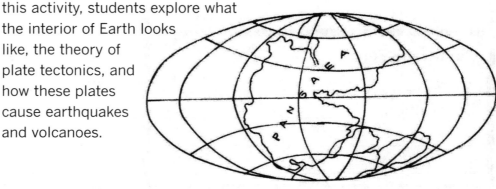

1. Have students fill out a **K-W-L Chart (page 15)** about plate tectonics. Ask: *What is plate tectonics? What do you know about the supercontinent Pangaea? What is continental drift?* Explain to students that scientists believe that about 200 million years ago, the surface of Earth consisted of one supercontinent called Pangaea that broke up and moved apart (continental drift) to form our seven continents.

2. Give each student two copies of the **Shifting Plates World Map reproducible (page 52)**. Have students use the first copy to cut out and glue together the continents to form an approximate picture of Pangaea in their notebooks. Ask them to write conclusions they draw from the completed map. (Note that the pieces will not fit together perfectly. The plates are shaped to reflect the recognizable outlines of today's continents.)

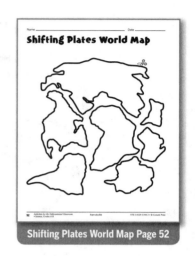

Shifting Plates World Map Page 52

3. Have them use the second copy to make a volcano and earthquake map. Tell students to map the locations of ten active volcanoes and ten historic earthquakes around the world. Direct them to draw colored lines showing the boundaries of the world's tectonic plates and create a map key of all the colors and symbols they used (such as red triangles for volcanoes and blue asterisks for earthquakes).

4. Distribute copies of the **Shifting Plates Choice Boards (page 53)** for students to complete independently or with a partner. Provide students with Internet access and other needed resources and materials. For the choice boards, you may differentiate instruction by checking off specific assignments for students to do, or have students choose their own.

Shifting Plates Choice Boards Page 53

5. Give students a **Time Log (page 16)** and a **Resources Organizer (page 17)** to help them keep organized and on task. Also encourage them to write a plan and a task list in their science notebooks to help them complete each part of their assignment.

6. Have students present their final products to the class. Encourage classmates to ask questions and complete a **Project Review (page 38)**.

Ideas for More Differentiation

Have more advanced learners do the following activity: *Besides a seismograph, what other device do you think could be developed to measure the strength of an earthquake? Design and sketch such a device. Explain how it would work, what it would measure, and how it would be more effective than a seismograph.*

Name _____ Date _____

Shifting Plates World Map

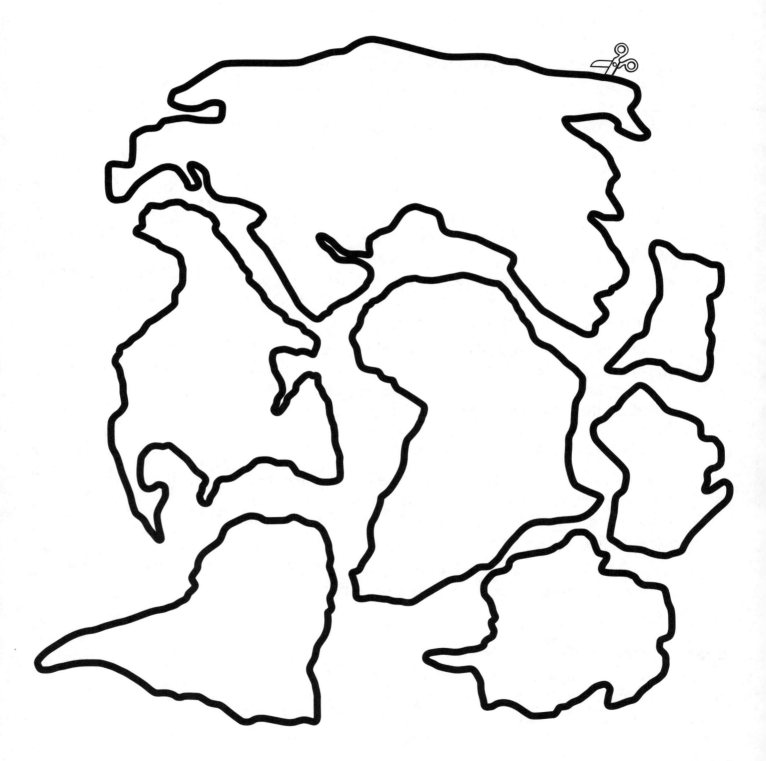

Reproducible   978-1-4129-5344-3 • © Corwin Press

Shifting Plates Choice Boards

Directions: Choose a topic and a product.

Topics

The different layers of Earth	Continental drift and plate tectonics theory	Types of movement at the plate boundaries: *divergent, convergent, transform*
Plate tectonics and the formation of mountains, earthquakes, and volcanoes	Types of volcanoes: *fissure, shield, ash-cinder, composite, dome, caldera*	The "Ring of Fire"
Earthquake safety and preparation	Historic earthquakes and volcanic eruptions	Detecting and predicting the movement of Earth's plates

Products

Diagrams and maps with labels	Pictures and drawings	Models with description cards
Short story or poem	Poster or brochure	Board game or card game
Children's book	Newspaper article	Free choice

Hazard Hunters

Standards

Earth and Space Science—Understand structure of the earth system.
Science in Personal and Social Perspectives—Identify natural hazards; understand risks and benefits; understand science and technology in society.
Unifying Concepts and Processes—Understand systems, order, and organization; understand evidence, models, and explanation; understand change, constancy, and measurement; understand form and function.

Objectives

Students will learn about the purposes and functions of the Federal Emergency Management Agency (FEMA).
Students will create products that promote public safety and awareness of natural hazards/disasters.

Materials

Public Safety Expert reproducibles
Time Log reproducible
Internet access and research materials about natural hazards
science notebooks

Every day communities around the world must deal with a variety of natural hazards and natural disasters that take a toll on human lives and property. In an effort to help alleviate and eliminate the impact of hazardous conditions, teams of scientists and researchers study both geologic and atmospheric hazards and their impact on society, including meteorologists, climatologists, geologists, social scientists, psychologists, and government agencies such as FEMA (Federal Emergency Management Agency) and USGS (United States Geological Survey). In this activity, students learn about different natural hazards and develop educational materials that help teach public awareness and safety in the event of a natural disaster.

1. Conduct a "brainstorming bash" with students in which they share their

knowledge and ideas about natural hazards and how to keep safe from them. Ask: *What is a natural hazard? What is the difference between an atmospheric hazard and a geologic hazard? What is the difference between a natural hazard and a natural disaster? List some natural hazards and how to protect yourself from them.*

2. Assign individual students, pairs, or trios a natural hazard from the following list, or have students choose one: *earthquakes, volcanoes, hurricanes, tsunamis, tornadoes, floods, landslides, avalanches, wildfires, droughts, blizzards, fog, severe thunderstorms.*

3. Distribute copies of **Public Safety Expert reproducibles (pages 56–57)**. For Part 1, have students research their natural hazard using reliable Web sites (such as *www.naturalhazards.org*) and other resources. For Part 2, encourage students to write an outline of their plan in their science notebooks before they begin preparing each part of their presentation. ▶

Public Safety Expert: Part 1 Page 56

4. Monitor students' progress as they work. Encourage students to use a **Time Log (page 16)** and their notebooks to help them keep organized ▶ and on task.

5. Provide time for students to share their presentations with the class. Encourage classmates to take notes about what they see and hear during the presentation, ask questions afterward, and give feedback about what they've learned and what they liked.

Time Log Page 16

Ideas for More Differentiation

- Beginning Mastery: Have students use a **Venn diagram (page 74)** to compare and contrast the terms *natural hazard* and *natural disaster*. Have them list and discuss any natural hazards and natural disasters that have occurred nearby or have been reported in the news.

- Approaching Mastery: Have students investigate and report on how the following federal agencies help protect the public from natural hazards and natural disasters: Federal Emergency Management Agency (FEMA), National Aeronautics and Space Administration (NASA), National Oceanic and Atmospheric Administration (NOAA), National Weather Service (NWS), United States Geological Survey (USGS).

- High Degree of Mastery: Challenge students to design and create a model of a building that can withstand a strong earthquake, flood, or tornado. Have them present their model to the class.

Name _____ Date _____

Public Safety Expert: Part 1

As a natural hazard prevention expert, you have been called by the Federal Emergency Management Agency (FEMA). Research your assigned hazard and answer the following questions for FEMA.

1. You are assigned to what kind of hazard?

_____

2. What time of year does this natural hazard usually occur?

_____

3. Describe your natural hazard. What causes it? What makes it hazardous?

_____

_____

4. In which parts of the United States and around the world does this type of natural hazard usually occur?

_____

_____

5. How can the public prepare for this natural hazard to prevent it from turning into a natural disaster?

_____

_____

6. List some examples of your natural hazard that have occurred in the past. What damage did it cause?

_____

_____

7. What efforts are people already making to reduce this hazard?

_____

978-1-4129-5344-3 • © *Corwin Press*

Public Safety Expert: Part 2

Thanks to you, FEMA now has all the information they need about your natural hazard, and they've decided that they need you in the field. You are allowed to pick any town where your hazard has turned into a natural disaster in the past.

1. First, you need to tell your FEMA officer where you are going:

   I have chosen to go to _____ to work in the field because my natural hazard, _____, has happened there and turned into a natural disaster on this date: _____.

2. Now that you've decided where to go, you need to figure out how to help the community. Provide them with the following information as part of a poster, a safety booklet, a public service announcement (PSA) for radio or television, or a video presentation.

   • Tell the community about the natural hazard. Describe the hazard, how it forms, and why it is a danger to the community. Include at least one labeled picture or drawing.

   • Provide a checklist of items to put in an evacuation kit. Also provide a list of items to put in a survival kit in case people can't get out of the area.

   • Draw a map of the town showing evacuation routes and emergency public shelters.

   • Develop an emergency communications plan.

   • Explain how to help children, people with disabilities, and injured individuals during the crisis. Also explain how to help pets and other animals in distress.

   • Summarize the importance of practicing the plan and keeping updated and informed.

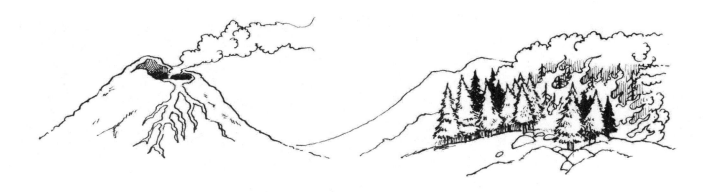

The Heat Is On

Strategy
Center activity

Standards
Science as Inquiry—Ability to conduct scientific inquiry.
Earth and Space Science—Understand structure of the earth system.
Science in Personal and Social Perspectives—Understand populations, resources, and environments; identify natural hazards; understand risks and benefits; understand science and technology in society.
History and Nature of Science—Understand the nature of science.
Unifying Concepts and Processes—Understand systems, order, and organization; understand evidence, models, and explanation.

Objective
Students will explore science centers to learn more about global warming, what causes it, how it affects the earth, and ways to stop it from happening.

Materials
K-W-L Chart reproducible
Time Log reproducible
Resources Organizer reproducible
Article Analysis reproducible
Cause and Effect Map reproducible
desktop science centers (trifold foam board, construction paper pockets, task cards)
supplies for each center as described on pages 60–61

Global warming is an increase in the average temperature of the earth's atmosphere due to an increase in the amount of carbon dioxide and other greenhouse gases, caused primarily by human activities such as deforestation and burning of fossil fuels. Global warming affects our climate, which can cause a rise in sea levels and an increase in extreme weather conditions such as floods, hurricanes, tornadoes, droughts, and heat waves.

For this activity, students work in science centers to learn more about global warming

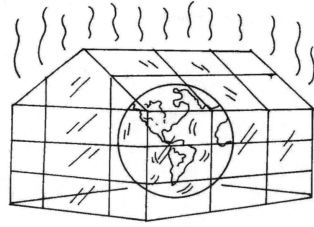

and how it affects the earth. Use the directions on pages 60–61 to set up your science centers. Make desktop centers using trifold foam board and construction paper pockets, including a pocket of task cards for directions and one or more pockets for reproducibles. In each center, place a box of other supplies that students need to complete the activities.

1. Have students fill out a **K-W-L Chart (page 15)** with what they already know about global warming and what they would like to know about it. Ask: *What is global warming? What causes it? How does it affect our climate and weather?*

K-W-L Chart Page 15

2. Have students rotate through the Global Warming Centers. Assign a starting point for each student or have them choose their own starting point. You may have all students complete all the activities in the centers, or assign specific activities to certain students. You may also want to have some students work with a partner or in small groups.

3. Have students complete a **Time Log (page 16)** as they work through the centers. This will help them stay on task, as well as give you an ongoing assessment of their progress.

4. Encourage students to complete a **Resources Organizer (page 17)** as they conduct research. After they list each resource on their organizer, have them write the resource number (e.g., *B1, M/N1, W1*) next to each fact in their notes.

Resources Organizer Page 17

Ideas for More Differentiation

- Beginning Mastery: Have students write a list of facts or draw a cartoon strip that shows what they know about global warming, its effects, and how it might be prevented.

- Approaching Mastery: Have students use the data from the Global Center 5: Energy Conservation questionnaire to construct a graph showing how their classmates and their families use energy.

- High Degree of Mastery: Challenge students to design an experiment to prove that floating ice does not cause a significant rise in sea levels. Have them research what causes sea levels to rise and then draw a diagram to go with their experiment.

Global Warming Centers

Global Center 1: What Is Global Warming?

Materials: Internet access and other references about global warming, Article Analysis reproducibles, Cause and Effect Maps, writing paper or science notebooks

Activities:

Article Analysis Page 62

- Find at least three different articles (from Web sites, newspapers, magazines) about global warming, and fill out an **Article Analysis (page 62)** about each one.

- Research the causes and effects of global warming, and then complete a **Cause and Effect Map (page 63)** to show what you've learned.

- Write a short essay about global warming. Explain what it is, its causes, and how it affects the earth. Include pictures and charts.

Global Center 2: Greenhouse Living

Materials: Internet access and other references about the greenhouse effect; large, clear glass jars with lids; small thermometers (smaller than the jars); soil; measuring cups; index cards, drawing paper, writing paper and science notebooks

Activities:

- Research facts about the greenhouse effect, and summarize what you've learned. Draw and label a diagram to go with your summary.

- Write a fictional story that explains how life on Earth would be different if there were no greenhouse effect.

- Use materials at this station to make a working model of the greenhouse effect. Include a description card and a drawing or diagram to go with your model.

Global Center 3: Sea Level Change

Materials: Internet access and other references about global warming and its affect on sea level, world map, writing paper or science notebooks

Activities:

- Research and write a summary about how global warming can cause a rise in sea level. Then refer to the map and make a list of ten major coastal cities that would be affected by a rise in sea level.

- How would marine animals be affected by a change in sea level? Is there anyway to prevent these changes? Write a narrative piece from the perspective of a sea creature.

- Pretend you live in a coastal city affected by a rise in sea level due to global warming. Write a story to tell the next generation what happened. What did you see? Did the water rise quickly or slowly? What effects did it have on your family, neighborhood, and community? How did you and other people handle the situation?

Global Center 4: Energy Alternatives

Materials: Internet access and other references about alternative energy sources, writing paper or science notebooks, drawing paper, markers, colored pencils, scissors, glue

Activities:

Research and list several alternative energy sources, and write at least three facts about each source. Then complete one or more of the following activities.

- Make a collage of pictures showing a variety of alternative energy sources. Use pictures from the Internet, magazines, and newspapers; or draw your own pictures.

- Choose one of the alternative energy sources and write a news report about why you think it's the best one.

- Prepare a debate with another student about which alternative energy source would be the best for the United States and why.

Global Center 5: Energy Conservation

Materials: Internet access and other references about energy conservation, writing paper or science notebooks, drawing paper, markers, colored pencils

Activities:

- Write a list of ten things you can do to conserve energy.

- Design a questionnaire to discover how your classmates and their families use energy. Use that data to write a news article about how to conserve energy.

- Design and create a magazine about energy conservation. Include informative articles, pictures, editorials, and advertisements. Be sure your magazine explains the connection between energy conservation and global warming.

Name _____ Date _____

Article Analysis

Title: _____ Author: _____

Source: _____ Date Published: _____

1. What is the main idea of this article?

_____

_____

_____

2. Who was involved in the situation?

_____

3. Where and **when** did it happen?

_____

4. How was the situation resolved?

_____

_____

_____

5. Why do you think this article was written? Do you agree with the author? Why?

_____

_____

_____

Important Vocabulary Words from the Article

Word: _____ Definition: _____

Word: _____ Definition: _____

Word: _____ Definition: _____

Name _____ Date _____

Cause and Effect Map

Directions: Write a cause in each triangle. Write the effects on each side of the cause.

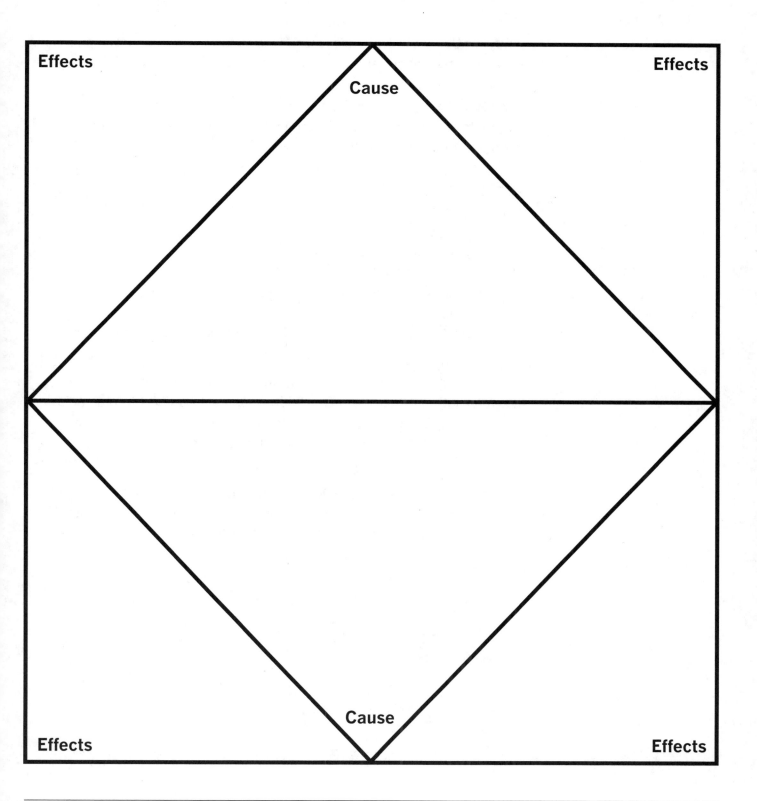

Effects

Cause

Effects

Effects

Cause

Effects

Planets, Planets Everywhere!

Strategies

Jigsaw

Choice board

Standards

Earth and Space Science—Understand Earth in the solar system.
History and Nature of Science—Understand science as a human endeavor; understand the history of science.
Unifying Concepts and Processes—Understand systems, order, and organization; understand evidence, models, and explanation.

Objective

Students will learn about the planets in our solar system and create products to show what they've learned.

Materials

K-W-L Chart reproducible
Planet Expert reproducible
Solar System Choice Board reproducible
Project Review reproducible
Internet access and other resources about our solar system
science notebooks
craft supplies and other materials for the choice-board assignments

Our solar system consists of the sun and all the objects that orbit it. Until August 24, 2006, our solar system had nine planets; on that day, the International Astronomical Union (IAU) reclassified Pluto as a "dwarf planet." Now there are only eight official planets in our solar system. In this activity, students will learn more about the solar system and create products to show what they've learned.

1. Have students fill out a **K-W-L Chart (page 15)** with what they already know about the solar system and what they would like to know about it. Invite students to share their ideas.

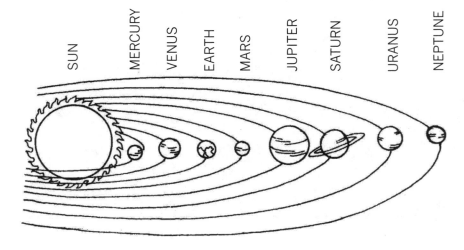

2. Divide the class into groups of eight, and assign a different planet to each group member. Then distribute copies of the **Planet Expert reproducible (page 66)**, and jigsaw students, having those assigned the same planet get together to research and answer the questions.

3. Have students return to their original base group and share the information written on their Planet Expert worksheet. Encourage group members to take notes in their science notebooks and update their K-W-L Charts as they listen to the information.

Planet Expert Page 66

4. Then distribute copies of the **Solar System Choice Board reproducible (page 67)**. Have students work independently or with a partner to complete the assignments. Provide any supplies that students need, or have students bring their own supplies from home. Encourage students to use their science notebooks to sketch ideas, take notes, and write to-do lists.

5. Provide time for students to share their completed projects with classmates. Then have the class complete a **Project Review (page 38)** for each project they review.

Ideas for More Differentiation

• Approaching Mastery: Have students imagine that NASA wants to build an orbiting space hotel. They will choose the planet they think is best for the hotel and defend their choice in a letter to NASA.

• High Degree of Mastery: Have students prepare and present a news report on one of the following topics: *Cepheid variables, supernovae, dark matter, cosmic background radiation, black holes, red shift.*

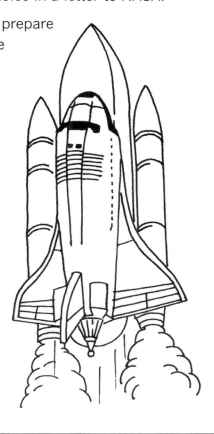

Project Review Page 38

Planet Expert

My planet is: _____

Position in the Solar System: _____

Size: _____

Who Discovered It and When: _____

_____

Average Surface Temperature: _____

Length of Day and Year: _____

Number of Satellites: _____

Physical Description: _____

_____

_____

Fascinating Facts: _____

_____

_____

Picture:

Solar System Choice Board

Directions: Complete at least three assignments from the choice board.

Write a real or fictitious interview with an astronaut. Include at least ten questions and answers about the space program and space travel. 	Write a fictional story or diary entries about space travel near, through, or inside a black hole. 	Use computer graphics or art supplies to make a model of the solar system. Include labels and description cards. 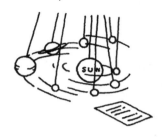
Draw a diagram or make a model of your own space shuttle. Include labels and descriptions. 	Your choice! Let's talk about it! 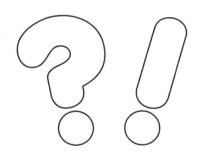	Create a poster for a movie about space exploration. Include planets, the sun, the moon, and other celestial bodies. 
Write a news article about the Arecibo radio dish in Puerto Rico. Include a message you would like to send from that device. 	Create a children's book or comic book about riding on a comet in space. Include facts about a famous comet. 	Create a solar system board game with fact cards about planets and other celestial bodies. 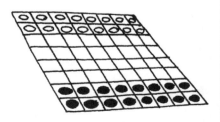

Star Struck

Standards

Earth and Space Science—Understand Earth in the solar system.
Unifying Concepts and Processes—Understand systems, order, and organization.

Objective

Students will explore the history and locations of constellations.

Materials

Star Struck reproducible
strips of paper
calculators

On a clear night, observers can see hundreds of stars that form constellations in the night sky. *Constellations* are arrangements of stars named by astronomers, poets, and even farmers throughout time. They appear in the form of shapes that are mostly named after mythological animals, creatures, and heroes. The real purpose of constellations is to give us *mnemonics*, or memory tools, for identifying and remembering the names of specific stars in the sky. For example, if you see three bright stars in a row on a winter's night, you might realize that they are part of the constellation *Orion* (named after a Greek hunter). This can help us recall specific names of all the stars in that constellation.

Although most of the constellations were named long ago, many of them have been redefined so that every star in the sky is in exactly one constellation. Today, the International Astronomical Union (IAU) officially recognizes 88 constellations in our celestial sphere, including the 12 constellations of the zodiac.

1. Invite volunteers to say the names of the 12 zodiac signs as you record the correct responses on the board (*Capricorn, Aquarius, Pisces, Aries, Taurus, Gemini, Cancer, Leo, Virgo, Libra, Scorpio, Sagittarius*). Then have students raise their hand when they hear you say the sign of their birth month, and record that number using tally marks. Ask: *What do you know about these zodiac signs? How are they associated with stars in the sky?* (The 12 signs of the zodiac are associated with constellations of stars that are along the pathway of the sun as it moves across the sky each year.)

2. Write the names of the following constellations on strips of paper, and have students randomly choose one: *Andromeda, Antlia, Aquarius, Aquila, Ara, Aries, Auriga, Boötes, Cancer, Canis Major, Capricorn, Carina, Cassiopeia, Centaurus, Cepheus, Cetus, Coma Berenices, Corona Borealis, Corvus, Crater, Crux, Cygnus, Delphinus, Draco, Eridanus, Gemini, Hercules, Hydra, Leo, Lepus, Libra, Lupus, Lyra, Ophiuchus, Orion, Pegasus, Perseus, Pisces, Piscis Austrinus, Puppis, Sagitta, Sagittarius, Scorpius, Taurus, Triangulum, Ursa Major, Ursa Minor, Vela, Virgo.*

3. Give each student a copy of the **Star Struck reproducible (page 70)** to complete. Provide Internet access and other resources for students to use for research. Encourage students to write an outline of their ideas in their science notebook before joining their group to work on the final product.

4. Place students in groups of mixed abilities and various talents. Have students share their research and select a constellation for the brochure. Tell the groups they will be making a travel brochure to entice humans to visit the constellation. Some students will write the text, some will do the design, and others will create or find pictures.

5. Display the brochures for all to see. Guide a discussion about which constellations students would like to visit.

Star Struck Page 70

Star Struck

Directions: You are a travel agent at the Intergalactic Travel Agency. The travel agents are competing to see who can lure the most space travelers to their constellation. Make a travel brochure, a poster, a commercial, or any other product to convince people to visit your constellation. Include the following information.

1. What is the name of your constellation? Include any nicknames.

   _____

2. Where is your constellation located in the sky?

   _____

3. At what time of year is your constellation the most visible?

   _____

4. What are the names, positions, and colors of the brightest stars in your constellation?

   _____

   _____

   _____

5. What other celestial objects are near your constellation?

   _____

   _____

   _____

6. Write three more interesting facts about your constellation.

   _____

   _____

   _____

   _____

CHAPTER 3

Life Science

Biomes

Standards

Life Science—Understand populations and ecosystems; understand diversity and adaptations of organisms.
Science in Personal and Social Perspectives—Understand populations, resources, and environments.
Unifying Concepts and Processes—Understand systems, order, and organization; understand evidence, models, and explanation.

Strategies
Cooperative group learning

Structured project

Objectives

Students will identify, describe, and compare different biomes of the world.
Students will demonstrate their understanding of biomes by making visual representations.

Materials

Building Biomes reproducible
Venn Diagram reproducible
Resources Organizer reproducible
Project Review reproducible
Group Review reproducible
a blank world map
supplies for group reports and projects
science notebooks
science portfolios

A *biome* is a large region of ecosystems where plants and animals live in a specific climate and have adapted to that environment. Biomes are divided into two major groups: *terrestrial biomes* and *aquatic biomes*. In this activity, students research pairs of biomes, write a report about their findings, and make a model to accompany their report.

1. Write on the board *BIOME—animals, plants, climate, environment.* Have students use those words to come up with a definition for *biome*. Then draw a Venn diagram on the board, and write *polar bear* at the top of one circle and *grizzly bear* at the top of the other. Have students identify, describe, and compare the biomes of the two bears as you record their correct responses in the Venn diagram.

2. Divide the class into five groups, and assign a pair of biomes to each group as follows: *tundra vs. desert; boreal forest vs. temperate forest; tropical rain forest vs. grassland; mountains vs. shrubland; marine vs. freshwater*.

3. Give each group a copy of the reproducibles **Building Biomes (page 73)** and **Venn Diagram (page 74)** and a blank world map. Explain to students that they need to compare and contrast their two biomes, write a comprehensive report about them, and build an accompanying model.

4. Have groups decide who will do each part of the assignment and write their initials next to those tasks on the Building Biomes worksheet. Recommend that pairs work together on each task. Require that all members help build the final model.

5. Have students check off tasks as they complete them. Encourage them to write daily goals and a flowchart of progress in their science notebooks. Provide students with copies of the **Resources Organizer (page 17)** to record their resources. Have them store any work in progress in their portfolios.

6. Display finished projects around the classroom, and have students complete a **Project Review (page 38)** as they review each display. Have groups also complete a **Group Review (page 75)** to self-assess their performance.

Ideas for More Differentiation

- Beginning Mastery: Have students color a world map to show where all the different biomes are located. Remind them to include a color key.

- Approaching Mastery: Invite students to find an animal or plant near their home or school that has developed a specific adaptation for that environment. Have them describe what would happen to the biome if that plant or animal disappeared.

- High Degree of Mastery: Have students use a computer graphing program and weather data to produce a *climatogram* for each biome—a graph of temperature vs. rainfall.

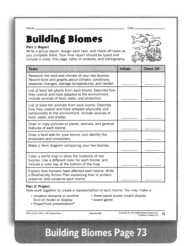

Building Biomes Page 73

Building Biomes

Part 1: Report

Write a group report. Assign each task, and check off tasks as you complete them. Your final report should be typed and include a cover, title page, table of contents, and bibliography.

Tasks	Initials	Check Off
Research the land and climate of your two biomes. Record facts and graphs about climatic conditions, seasonal changes, average temperatures, and rainfall.	_____	_____
List at least ten plants from each biome. Describe how they coexist and have adapted to the environment. Include sources of food, water, and protection.	_____	_____
List at least ten animals from each biome. Describe how they coexist and have adapted physically and behaviorally to the environment. Include sources of food, water, and shelter.	_____	_____
Draw or copy pictures of plants, animals, and general features of each biome.	_____	_____
Draw a food web for your biome, and identify the producers and consumers.	_____	_____
Make a Venn diagram comparing your two biomes.	_____	_____
Color a world map to show the locations of two biomes. Use a different color for each biome, and include a color key at the bottom of the map.	_____	_____
Explain how humans have affected each biome. Write a Biodiversity Action Plan explaining how to protect, preserve, and conserve each biome.	_____	_____

Part 2: Project

Now work together to create a representation of each biome. You may make a:

- shoebox diorama or another kind of model or display
- PowerPoint presentation®
- three-panel poster board display
- board game

Venn Diagram

Topic: _____

Topic: _____

Both

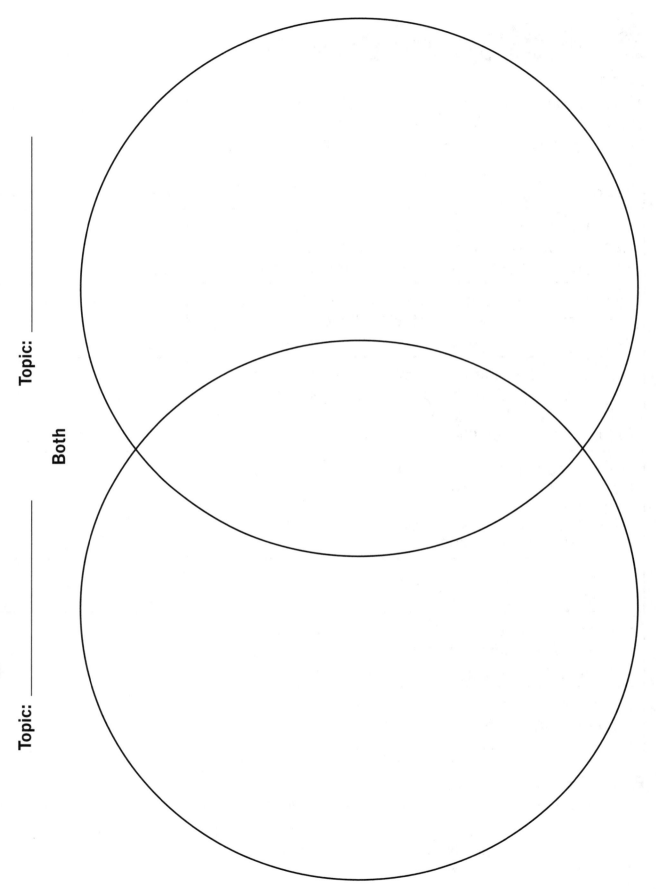

Reproducible

Name _____ Date _____

Group Review

Name of Project: _____

Group Members: _____

Directions: Circle a score for your group's
performance in each category.

Communication: 1   2   3   4   5
Sharing responsibilities: 1   2   3   4   5
Problem solving: 1   2   3   4   5
Overall teamwork: 1   2   3   4   5

What did you like best about being part of this group?

_____

_____

What do you think your group could have done better?

_____

_____

What did you like best about your role in the group?

_____

_____

What do you think you could have done better?

_____

_____

Other comments:

_____

_____

Body Systems

Strategies

Focus activity

Authentic task

Standards
Life Science—Understand structure and function in living systems. Science in Personal and Social Perspectives—Understand the importance of personal health; understand risks and benefits. Unifying Concepts and Processes—Understand systems, order, and organization; understand form and function.

Objective
Students will learn about the 12 major body systems and create medical pamphlets.

Materials
Body Systems Expert reproducible
Body Systems Pamphlet reproducible
Resources Organizer reproducible
butcher paper
large self-stick notes
books and other resources about the human body systems
science notebooks
sample pamphlets
trifolded paper or computer software to create pamphlets
colored pencils, markers, crayons
yarn

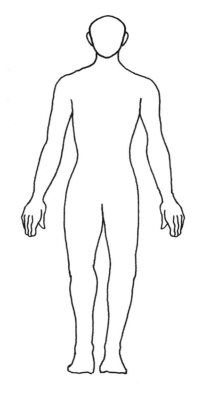

The human body is comprised of 12 major systems: *immune, digestive, nervous, endocrine, reproductive, urinary, respiratory, circulatory, lymphatic, skeletal, muscular, integumentary*. When any one of these systems malfunctions or fails, disease or death can occur. In this activity, students will explore these body systems, learn how the systems function independently and interdependently, research different diseases that can affect each system, and apply their knowledge by creating medical pamphlets.

1. In advance, prepare a life-sized outline of a human body on butcher paper. Display the outline on a wall, as the center of an upcoming class exhibit.

2. Direct students' attention to the human outline, and ask them to imagine themselves as a little germ that has just entered the body. Prompt them to list the 12 major body systems the germ could infect. Write correct responses on self-stick notes, and invite volunteers to stick them on the outline in the appropriate places.

3. Divide the class into teams of two or three, and assign a different body system to each team. Give each team a copy of the **Body Systems Expert** and **Body Systems Pamphlet reproducibles (pages 78–79)**. Explain to students that they will create a medical pamphlet about their system—its location in the body, which organs are involved, how it works, and how to keep it healthy. Provide teams with Internet access, computer software, research materials, and other needed materials to complete the assignment.

Body Systems Expert Page 78

4. Have students use their science notebook and a **Resources Organizer (page 17)** to help them keep track of their facts, ideas, and references. Have them submit a sketch or outline of their pamphlet for your approval before they start their final product. Encourage them to review sample pamphlets for more ideas.

5. In addition to their pamphlets, have students draw their assigned system in the human outline on the wall. Post the finished pamphlets on the wall next to the outline, and use yarn to connect the pamphlets to the corresponding system drawn in the outline.

6. Invite students to view the completed exhibit on the wall, and generate a list of questions for students to answer about the display. You might also make photocopies of the pamphlets for each student.

Ideas for More Differentiation

- Beginning Mastery: Have students choose a sport or activity that they enjoy and list all the body systems used during that activity.

- Approaching Mastery: Have students create a model of one of the body systems.

- High Degree of Mastery: Have students research the effects of one of the following health hazards on the human body and create before and after models for comparison: cigarettes, drugs, alcohol, lack of exercise, unhealthy diet, poor hygiene.

Name _____ Date _____

Body Systems Expert

1. What is your assigned body system? _____

2. What is the job of this body system? _____

_____

_____

3. What organs are involved? On a separate page, draw a diagram of the system.

_____

_____

4. How does this system work? How does it work with other systems in the body?

_____

_____

5. What happens to the body if this system stops functioning properly?

_____

_____

6. What are some diseases and disorders that affect this system? List at least three. Describe their symptoms, how they affect the body, and possible treatments.

_____

_____

_____

7. Name some preventative measures that keep this system healthy.

_____

_____

_____

Name _____ Date _____

Body Systems Pamphlet

Directions: Make a medical pamphlet to teach the public about your assigned body system. Use the following guidelines and facts from your Body Systems Expert sheet.

1. Include the following information in your pamphlet:

- A definition of your body system
- Its role in the body
- How it works
- How it affects other systems in the body
- Diseases and disorders that affect its function
- Possible treatments and cures for those diseases and disorders
- Preventative measures that can be taken to keep the system healthy

2. Before you start making your pamphlet, determine the following:

- What is the purpose of your pamphlet? Who is your target audience?
- What captivating headline will you use?
- What facts will you include? In what order will you present them?
- What pictures, drawings, and diagrams will you include? What about captions?
- What is the layout of your pamphlet? What will you put on the front and back?
- What font style and size will you use?
- Where will you put boldface, underlined, or italicized words?
- What other visual features will you include?
- What is your team's logo or name? Where will you put it on your pamphlet?

3. Make an outline or sketch of your pamphlet. Get your teacher's approval before you begin the final product. As you make your pamphlet, consider the following:

- Make sure your pamphlet is not too crowded with text.
- Leave some space in between sections, and break up the text with pictures.
- Avoiding using long words and slang whenever possible.
- Make sure that all of your facts are correct.
- Check the spelling, and proofread your pamphlet carefully.

Model DNA

Strategies
Energizing partners

Structured project

Standards
Life Science—Understand structure and function in living systems; understand reproduction and heredity.

Unifying Concepts and Processes—Understand systems, order, and organization; understand evidence, models, and explanation.

Objective
Students will make a model of DNA to show their understanding of its structure and function.

Materials
Model DNA reproducible
science notebooks
research materials about DNA, genes, and chromosomes
fishing line
uncooked tube and wagon-wheel pasta
pipe cleaners (red, green, purple, yellow)
tape

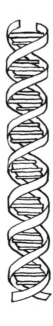

The genetic code of all living organisms is in strands of *DNA*, deoxyribonucleic acid, packed as pairs inside *chromosomes*. The strands have thousands of pairs of molecular building blocks joined by hydrogen bonds and entwined in a double helix. The building blocks, *nucleotides*, consist of alternating *sugar-phosphates* forming a backbone for four *nucleobases*: adenine (A), thymine (T), cytosine (C), and guanine (G). Each base on one strand forms a bond with its complementary base on the other strand to make a *base pair* (A with T; C with G). A *gene* is a hereditary unit with a specific sequence of nucleotides in the DNA of a chromosome. Genes determine the traits of an organism. In this activity, students make a DNA model to show their understanding of its genetic structure and function.

1. Have students form "energizing partners" and take turns sharing their knowledge of DNA's structure, function, and location in the body. Encourage students to take notes in their science notebooks. Then ask: *What is DNA?* (hereditary material passed down from parent to offspring) *What does DNA look like?* (a twisting double helix) *Where can you find DNA?* (in the nucleus and mitochondria of cells) *What are genes?* (specific units of DNA that determine an organism's traits)

2. Explain to students that they will be making a model of DNA. Have partners research the structure of DNA and complete a copy of the **Model DNA reproducible (page 82)**. Then have a class discussion about the structure and composition of a DNA double helix.

3. Write the DNA Key on the board. Show how to build the model: string pasta onto fishing line, alternating tube pasta (representing phosphate) and wagon-wheel pasta (representing sugar). Make two identical strands. Twist "complementary pairs" of pipe cleaner (red/green; purple/yellow) to make "base pairs" attached to wagon-wheel pasta across from each other, forming a double helix.

Model DNA Page 82

DNA Key

tubular pasta = phosphate	green pipe cleaner = adenine
wagon-wheel pasta = sugar	purple pipe cleaner = guanine
red pipe cleaner = thymine	yellow pipe cleaner = cytosine

4. Distribute supplies to each student pair: 2 strands of fishing line; 22 pieces of tube pasta; 20 pieces of wagon-wheel pasta; 20 pipe cleaners of each color—red, green, purple, yellow. Then have partners build their own DNA gene that includes three to ten nucleotides (three to five base pairs). Remind them that each nucleotide consists of a sugar, a phosphate, and a base. Suggest that they tape the bottom of their fishing line to their desk so the pasta doesn't fall off while they build the DNA.

5. When models are complete, have students write their gene's genetic code (order of base pairs) on the board to create a class DNA sequence. Have each pair use a different color to write their code so each gene stands out in the DNA sequence.

6. Create a class model of your DNA helix by tying the genes together. Invite two volunteers to hold and twist the DNA model to form a double helix of DNA. Hang it from the ceiling.

Ideas for More Differentiation

- Beginning Mastery: Use magnetic letters to show the sequence of one strand of DNA; and have students show the corresponding strand.

- Approaching Mastery: Have one student write the sequence for one strand of a DNA and draw the corresponding picture; have a partner write and draw the complementary strand.

- High Degree of Mastery: Have students research the difference between DNA and RNA. Then have them write the messenger RNA that would complement the class's DNA strand.

Model DNA

Directions: Answer the following questions. Use research materials to help you.

1. Where are chromosomes located in eukaryotic cells?

_____

2. What is the definition of *DNA*? How is DNA related to chromosomes?

_____

_____

3. What is a *nucleotide*? Describe it.

_____

_____

4. What is a *base pair*? Describe the relationship between the bases thymine and adenine and the bases guanine and cytosine.

_____

_____

5. Draw the basic structure of a DNA helix.

6. What are *genes*? How are they related to chromosomes?

_____

_____

7. What is the relationship between an organism's genes and its traits?

_____

_____

Phenotype Family Tree

Standards
Life Science—Understand reproduction and heredity; understand diversity and adaptations of organisms.
Unifying Concepts and Processes—Understand evolution and equilibrium.

Objectives
Students will understand the difference between genotype and phenotype.
Students will describe and compare family traits and characteristics.

Materials
Phenotype Family Chart reproducible
construction paper
colored pencils or markers
glue

Strategies
Focus activity

Project

A person's *genotype* is the specific genetic makeup or blueprint of that individual, inherited from parents. The *phenotype* is the physical results or appearance of that genotype and the environment. A *trait* is a small part of the phenotype, such as eye color or foot size. In this activity, students will create a "phenotype family tree" of traits and participate in a collaborative Internet project about phenotypic traits.

1. Write the definition of *phenotype* on the board. Invite volunteers to tell about physical features in their ancestry that are family traits. Ask: *What features do you have in common with people in your family? What is different about how you look? How do you think traits are passed down through families?*

2. Explain to students that they will create a family tree of phenotypic traits. You might choose to give students the option of using their own family, a historic family, a celebrity family, an animal family, or a fictitious family (e.g., a storybook family).

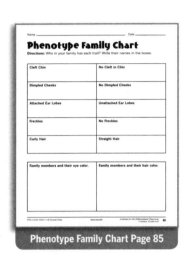

Phenotype Family Chart Page 85

3. Have students complete a **Phenotype Family Chart (page 85)** to gather information about their family. Then have them use that information along with pictures to create a phenotypic family tree on construction paper.

4. Display students' family trees in a "forest of families," and invite classmates to identify the physical features that are similar in each generation. Encourage students to also compare the phenotypic traits of different families and look for similarities.

5. Extend the activity by having students participate in an Internet-based collaborative project in which students complete surveys about the phenotypic traits of classmates and schoolmates, which are then compared to the traits of other students around the world. Assign graphing activities based on the data generated from this site. Go to the Center for Innovation in Engineering and Science Education Web site at: *www.k12science.org/curriculum/genproj.*

Ideas for More Differentiation

- Beginning Mastery: Have students define the terms *dominant* and *recessive*. Ask them to identify which traits in their family tree are dominant and which ones are recessive.

- Approaching Mastery: Have students use a Punnett Square (a chart showing all possible gene combinations) to show how someone in their family acquired one of their traits.

- High Degree of Mastery: Have students research the nature vs. nurture controversy and discover how scientists compare identical twins raised apart to investigate the issue. Then have them propose their own experiment to investigate the issue of hereditary vs. environmental influences. Remind them to include a hypothesis in their write-up.

Phenotype Family Chart

Directions: Who in your family has each trait? Write their names in the boxes.

Cleft Chin	No Cleft in Chin
Dimpled Cheeks	No Dimpled Cheeks
Attached Ear Lobes	Unattached Ear Lobes
Freckles	No Freckles
Curly Hair	Straight Hair

Family members and their eye color.	Family members and their hair color.

Giraffe Genetics

Strategies

Focus activity

Simulation

Standards

Life Science—Understand reproduction and heredity; understand diversity and adaptations of organisms.
Unifying Concepts and Processes—Understand evolution and equilibrium.

Objectives

Students will use pennies to determine the traits of a giraffe and draw a picture of the resulting offspring.
Students will understand the differences between *genotype* and *phenotype, dominant* and *recessive,* and *homozygous* and *heterozygous.*

Materials

Giraffe Traits reproducible
Giraffe Genetics reproducible
colored pencils or thin markers
pennies
tracing paper
scissors (optional)
glue (optional)

All mammals have two copies (alleles) of every gene—one from the mother and one from the father. When both copies of the gene are identical (the same allele), the gene is called *homozygous;* when both are different, the gene is called *heterozygous.* The genotype for each pair of alleles is written with uppercase and lowercase letters—uppercase for the dominant allele, and lowercase for the recessive allele. The dominant allele is always written first, for example *Bb.*

The *phenotype* of a trait depends on whether the alleles for that trait are dominant or recessive. A *recessive phenotype* can only be expressed when both alleles are recessive for that trait, such as for blue eye color, written *bb.* A *dominant phenotype* can be expressed when only one or both alleles are dominant, such as for brown eye color, written *Bb* or *BB.* In this activity, students use pennies to determine the traits of two giraffes and draw a picture of the resulting offspring.

1. Write the following vocabulary terms in one column on the board, and write the corresponding definitions in another column in mixed order. Invite students to match each term with the correct definition: *recessive trait* (not expressed; you can't see it); *dominant trait* (expressed; you can see it); *genotype* (the genes of an organism); *phenotype* (physical appearance); *homozygous* (pair of identical alleles for the same gene); *heterozygous* (pair of different alleles for the same gene).

2. Give each student a copy of the **Giraffe Traits reproducible (page 88)**, and review the meaning of *alleles* and how genes are passed down to offspring. Have students complete the chart by coloring the giraffe pictures as indicated. You may also use a giraffe picture as an example to discuss with students.

3. Then have students use their Giraffe Traits reproducible to help them complete the **Giraffe Genetics reproducibles (pages 89–90)**. For students who are not comfortable drawing freehand, provide them with tracing paper so they may trace the parts shown on the Giraffe Traits chart, or provide them with photocopies of those pictures to cut and paste.

4. Display students' results. Have classmates identify the dominate and recessive traits in the baby giraffes.

Giraffe Traits Page 88

Ideas for More Differentiation

- Have students choose two of their classmates' giraffes and figure out the offspring of those two giraffes—the next generation.

- For a greater challenge, have students investigate the meaning of the following terms and explain how these factors can affect the phenotype of the giraffe offspring: *incomplete dominance, co-dominance, wild-type allele, mutant allele*.

- Beginning Mastery: Have students determine the traits of one possible offspring and draw a picture of that giraffe.

- Approaching Mastery: Have students determine the traits of four different offspring and draw pictures of those giraffes.

- High Degree of Mastery: Have students determine the traits of at least ten possible offspring and list them in a family tree.

Name _____   Date _____

Giraffe Traits

Directions: Complete this chart to help you determine what your baby giraffe will look like for *Giraffe Genetics*. Remember, the genotype for each trait is a combination of two alleles for that gene, one from each parent. Uppercase letters stand for dominant alleles; lowercase letters stand for recessive alleles.

Eye Shape  Circle (C) Triangle (c)	**Eye Color**  Green (G) Blue (g) (color me) (color me)
Ear Shape  Round (E) Pointed (e)	**Mouth Shape**  Curved (V) Straight (v)
Freckles  Present (F) Absent (f)	**Nose Color**  Pink (P) Black (p) (color me) (color me)
Neck Length  Long (N) Short (n)	**Mane Length**  Short (M) Long (m)
Mane Style 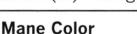 Curly (S) Straight (s)	**Mane Color**  Black (B) Brown (b) (color me) (color me)
Leg Length  Long (L) Short (l)	**Hide Color** 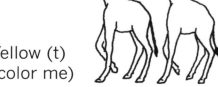 Tan (T) Yellow (t) (color me) (color me)

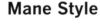

 Activities for the Differentiated Classroom • Science, Grades 6–8   Reproducible   978-1-4129-5344-3 • © Corwin Press

Name _____ Date _____

Giraffe Genetics, Part 1

Directions: For each trait, flip a coin to determine which allele is inherited from each parent, the dominant allele or the recessive allele. Flip the coin once for the mother. If it lands on heads, circle the dominant allele (the uppercase letter for that trait). If it lands on tails, circle the recessive allele (the lowercase letter for that trait). Repeat the process for the father. Then write the resulting genotype and phenotype for the baby that inherits those traits.

Trait	Mother's Allele		Father's Allele		Genotype of Baby	Phenotype of Baby
Eye Shape	C	c	C	c		
Eye Color	G	g	G	g		
Ear Shape	E	e	E	e		
Mouth Shape	V	v	V	v		
Freckles	F	f	F	f		
Nose Color	P	p	P	p		
Neck Length	N	n	N	n		
Mane Length	M	m	M	m		
Mane Style	S	s	S	s		
Mane Color	B	b	B	b		
Leg Length	L	l	L	l		
Hide Color	T	t	T	t		

Giraffe Genetics, Part 2

Directions: Draw the baby giraffe. Include all the phenotypic traits from *Giraffe Genetics, Part 1*. You may look back at the pictures on the *Giraffe Traits* chart to help you draw your giraffe.

Now determine whether the baby giraffe is male or female. Flip a coin once for the father only. If it lands on heads, he gives an X chromosome to the baby; if it lands on tails, he gives a Y chromosome. The mother will always give an X chromosome. For a female baby (XX), write the letter *F*; for a male baby (XY), write the letter *M*.

That's Debatable

Standards

Science as Inquiry—Understand about scientific inquiry.
Life Science—Understand reproduction and heredity; understand populations and ecosystems.
Science and Technology—Understand about science and technology.
Science in Personal and Social Perspectives—Understand populations, resources, and environments; understand risks and benefits; understand science and technology in society.
History and Nature of Science—Understand the nature of science.
Unifying Concepts and Processes—Understand evidence, models, and explanation.

Objectives

Students will research the pros and cons of a controversial medical treatment and participate in a class debate.

Materials

That's Debatable reproducible
Resources Organizer reproducible
Internet access and other reference materials about medical research
science notebooks
note cards

Heated debates always seem to surround advances in science. From the political arena to boardrooms and living rooms, decisions need to be made. In order to make informed decisions, people must know what they are arguing for and against. In this activity, students research both sides of a controversial medical treatment and use their research to prepare for and participate in a class debate.

1. Present the following information about Parkinson's disease (see box) to the class, and invite students to share their thoughts and opinions about each controversial treatment.

Actor Michael J. Fox, star of the *Back to the Future* movies, was diagnosed with Parkinson's disease in 1991. Parkinson's disease is a chronic, progressive disorder of the central nervous system and is the direct result of the loss of brain cells that produce *dopamine*, a chemical that helps the body control its movements. An estimated one million Americans, including Attorney General Janet Reno and former heavyweight champion Muhammad Ali, suffer from the disease, which has no known cause or cure. In addition to the traditional drugs and surgical procedures being used to treat the disease, the following experimental approaches are also being tested:

- *cloned animal cells*, such as pig brain cells, to replace the dwindling supply of human brain cells that produce dopamine

- *embryonic stem cells* (undifferentiated cells from days-old embryos, mostly from in vitro fertilization) to replace cells lost during the disease's progression

- *adult stem cells* collected from bone marrow (usually more difficult to use than embryonic stem cells) to replace cells lost during the disease's progression

2. Explain to students that they will be responsible for presenting a speech and participating in debate regarding a current scientific method or approach that is controversial. Then distribute copies of the **That's Debatable reproducible (page 94)**. Use the following list to assign a topic and position (pro or con) to each student, or have them choose their own:
   - stem cell research
   - cloning of humans
   - cloning of pets and other animals
   - gene therapy and genetic enhancement
   - genetically modified food, plants, animals
   - genetic testing of adults for determining predisposition to diseases
   - human organ transplantation
   - xenotransplantation—animal to human transplantation
   - embryo selection to predetermine gender of babies
   - nanotechnology—manipulating matter at atomic, molecular, and cellular levels
   - mandatory collection of DNA for a nationwide database

That's Debatable Page 94

3. As they gather information and prepare for their debate, have students use their science notebook to record information and organize their ideas. Encourage them to brainstorm approaches and discuss their ideas with classmates. Have them use a **Resources Organizer (page 17)** to help them keep track of their research materials. Provide them with note cards to organize and present their speech. Remind students that all of their suggestions and ideas must be supported by factual information. Provide time for them to practice their speech with a partner.

4. Before you start the debates, you may want to review proper conduct and behavior with the class. Encourage students to be respectful and supportive of each other.

5. Have students take turns presenting their speech to "Congress" (the class). Give each presenter time to refute/debate the arguments of their opponent. Encourage audience members to ask questions during the debate and to vote afterward.

Ideas for More Differentiation

Explain to students that a lot of scientific reality today was first dreamed up by science fiction writers long ago. Invite students to write their own science fiction story that involves a unique and unusual scientific idea. Then have them exchange stories with a classmate and discuss which ideas are most likely to end up becoming reality and why.

That's Debatable

Congress is considering a number of bills that will impact the scientific community. One of the bills is about your scientific approach. As an expert, you must advise Congress on how to vote on or amend the bill. Prepare and present a speech to convince Congress to vote in your favor.

Goal

Decide on the goal or purpose of your speech. What is your point of view? What do you hope to accomplish? How do you think you can reach that goal?

Research

Use the Internet and other reliable resources to find important facts and persuasive information to support your opinion. Include the following information:

- When and why was your method developed?
- How was the method developed, and how is it used today?
- Who will benefit from its use?
- What are the pros and cons, benefits, and side effects of this method?
- What are some misconceptions about its use?
- What are some statistics and results? Include testimonials from users.
- Include funding sources for research, development, testing, and usage.
- Write a description of the bill. Include any amendments you would like to add.

Organization

Organize the information for your speech. Decide what you will say and how you will respond to your opponent's arguments. Highlight important facts from your research. Write those facts on the front of note cards, and write your resources on the back. Number your note cards in the order in which you will present them. Write an outline of your speech, and include a captivating introduction and a powerful closing. Prepare visuals to help you persuade Congress to vote for your position.

Practice

Practice your speech in front of friends, family, classmates, and even in front of a mirror. If possible, tape-record or videotape yourself so you can self-critique and improve your performance. Remember, in order to persuade your audience, you must craft not only what you say, but also how you say it.

Presentation

Present your speech with confidence. Remember to look at your audience more than your notes, and make eye contact. Speak slowly, clearly, and with conviction.

Answer Key

ORIGINS OF LIFE (PAGE 47)

1. First evidence of life (~3,850 million years ago [mya])
2. Oldest fossils (~3,500 mya)
3. First evidence of soft-bodied animals (~900 mya)
4. The Cambrian Explosion (~530 mya)
5. First land plants and fish (~410 mya)
6. First reptiles (~250 mya)
7. First mammals and dinosaurs (~220 mya)
8. First birds (~150 mya)
9. First hominids (~5.2 mya)
10. First modern humans (~0.1 mya)

MASS REDUCTION OR EXTINCTION (PAGE 48)

1. Single-celled, soft-bodied animals (Precambrian, ~543 mya)
2. Reef-builders, shallow-water organisms (Cambrian, ~520 mya)
3. ~25% of marine invertebrate families (End Ordovician, ~443 mya)
4. ~50% of marine invertebrates (Late Devonian , ~364 mya)
5. ~90% of all species (End Permian, ~250 mya)
6. ~50% of marine invertebrate genera (Late Triassic, ~206 mya)
7. Dinosaurs, 60–80% of all species (End Cretaceous, ~65 mya)
8. Foraminifera, gastropods, sea urchins (Late Eocene, ~33 mya)
9. Plant-eating woodland Herbivores (Miocene, ~9 mya)
10. Mammals and birds over 45 lbs. (Late Pleistocene, ~0.1 mya)

THE CHANGING PLANET (PAGE 49)

1. The great oceans form (~4,200 mya)
2. Continents begin shifting (~3,100 mya)
3. Rodinia supercontinent forms (~1,100 mya)
4. Rodinia supercontinent breaks up (~700 mya)
5. Gondwana forms (~500 mya)
6. Great mountain ranges form (~425 mya)
7. Pangaea supercontinent forms (~280 mya)
8. Pangaea supercontinent breaks up (~200 mya)
9. Inland seas dry up (~20 mya)
10. Global ice ages begin (~2 mya)

MODEL DNA (POSSIBLE ANSWERS) (PAGE 82)

1. Eukaryotic chromosomes are located in the nucleus of a cell.
2. *DNA* stands for *deoxyribonucleic acid*; chromosomes are made up of DNA.
3. A *nucleotide* is a unit of DNA; it's a sugar-phosphate molecule attached to one of four nucleobases.
4. A *base pair* is a complementary pair of nucleobases; thymine and adenine are always paired together, as are guanine and cytosine.
5. Students should draw a ladder-like structure that consists of two strands of sugar-phosphate backbones connected with pairs of nulceobases (adenine with thymine; cytosine with guanine).

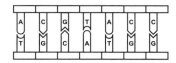

6. *Genes* are made up of DNA, and they are carried on the chromosomes.
7. An organism's genes determine its traits.

978-1-4129-5344-3

References

Dolan, C. (n.d.). *Constellations*. Retrieved October, 27, 2006 from the University of Wisconsin-Madison, Department of Astronomy Web site: http://www.astro.wisc .edu/~dolan/contstellations/.

Gregory, G. H. & Chapman, C. (2002). *Differentiated instructional strategies: One size doesn't fit all*. Thousand Oaks, CA: Corwin Press, Inc.

National Council for the Social Studies. (2002). *Expectations of excellence: Curriculum standards for social studies*. Silver Spring, MD: National Council for the Social Studies (NCSS).

National Council of Teachers of English and International Reading Association. (1996). *Standards for the English language arts*. Urbana, IL: National Council of Teachers of English (NCTE).

National Council of Teachers of Mathematics. (2005). *Principles and standards for school mathematics*. Reston, VA: National Council of Teachers of Mathematics (NCTM).

National Research Council. (2005). *National science education standards*. Washington, DC: National Academy Press.

PBS. (2001). *Evolution: Change: Deep time*. Retrieved October 27, 2006, from http://www.pbs.org/wgbh/evolution/change/deeptime/low_bandwidth.html.

Stevens Institute of Technology: The Center for Innovation in Engineering and Science Education. (2007). *Collaborative projects: Human genetics*. Retrieved October 27, 2006, from http://www.k12science.org/curriculum/genproj/.

Van Helden, A. (2004). *The biography of Galileo Galilei*. Retrieved October 27, 2006, from http://cnx.org/content/m11933/1.4/.